Evaluation of the Groundwater Flow Model for Southern Utah and Goshen Valleys, Utah, Updated to Conditions through 2011, with New Projections and Groundwater Management Simulations

By Lynette E. Brooks

In cooperation with the Southern Utah Valley Municipal Water Association

Open-File Report 2013–1171

U.S. Department of the Interior
U.S. Geological Survey

U.S. Department of the Interior
SALLY JEWELL, Secretary

U.S. Geological Survey
Suzette M. Kimball, Acting Director

U.S. Geological Survey, Reston, Virginia: 2013

For more information on the USGS—the Federal source for science about the Earth, its natural and living resources, natural hazards, and the environment, visit *http://www.usgs.gov* or call 1–888–ASK–USGS.

For an overview of USGS information products, including maps, imagery, and publications, visit *http://www.usgs.gov/pubprod*.

To order this and other USGS information products, visit *http://store.usgs.gov*.

Suggested citation:
Brooks, L.E, 2013, Evaluation of the groundwater flow model for southern Utah and Goshen Valleys, Utah, updated to conditions through 2011, with new projections and groundwater management simulations: U.S. Geological Survey Open-File Report 2013–1171, 35 p.

Contents

Figures

Tables

Conversion Factors and Datums

Inch/Pound to SI

Multiply	By	To obtain
Length		
foot (ft)	0.3048	meter (m)
mile (mi)	1.609	kilometer (km)
Area		
acre	4,047	square meter (m^2)
acre	0.4047	hectare (ha)
square mile (mi^2)	2.590	square kilometer (km^2)
Volume		
acre-foot (acre-ft)	1,233	cubic meter (m^3)
acre-foot (acre-ft)	0.001233	cubic hectometer (hm^3)
Flow rate		
acre-foot per year (acre-ft/yr)	1,233	cubic meter per year (m^3/yr)
acre-foot per year (acre-ft/yr)	0.001233	cubic hectometer per year (hm^3/yr)
foot per year (ft/yr)	0.3048	meter per year (m/yr)
gallon per minute (gal/min)	0.06309	liter per second (L/s)

Vertical coordinate information is referenced to the National Geodetic Vertical Datum of 1929 (NGVD 29).

Horizontal coordinate information is referenced to the North American Datum of 1983 (NAD 83).

Altitude, as used in this report, refers to distance above the vertical datum.

Wells by the Cadastral System of Land Subdivision

The well-numbering system used in Utah is based on the Cadastral system of land subdivision. The well-numbering system is familiar to most water users in Utah, and the well number shows the location of the well by quadrant, township, range, section, and position within the section. Well numbers for most of the State are derived from the Salt Lake Base Line and Meridian.

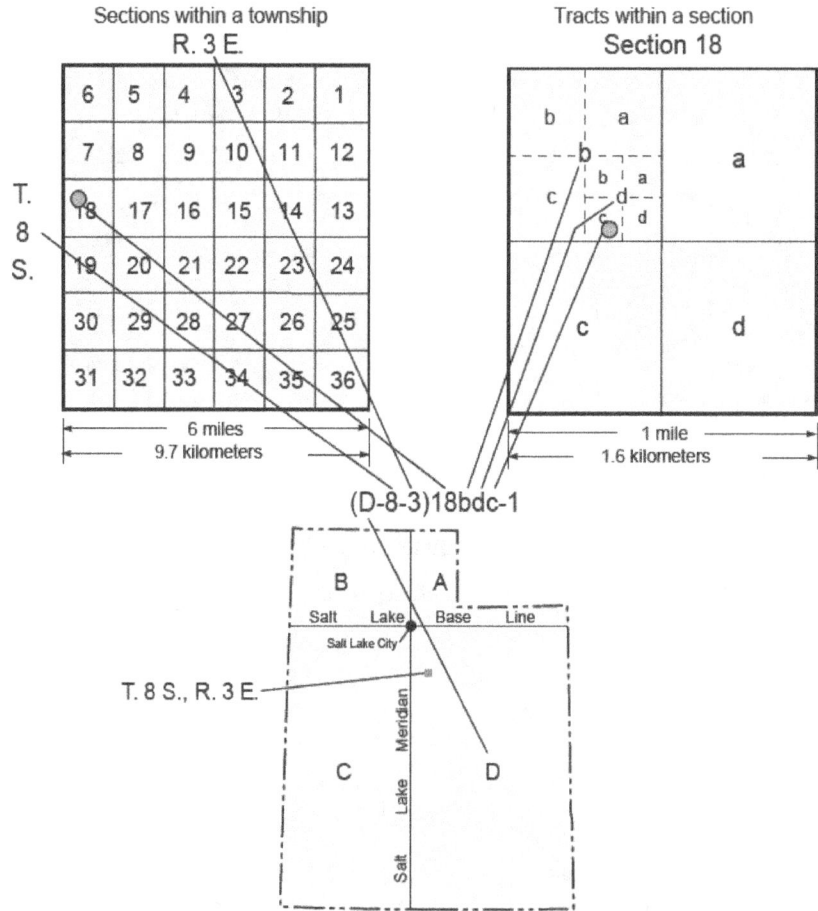

Surface-Water Sites— Downstream Order and Station Number

Since October 1, 1950, hydrologic-station records in U.S. Geological Survey reports have been listed in order of downstream direction along the main stream. All stations on a tributary entering upstream from a main-stream station are listed before that station. A station on a tributary entering between two main-stream stations is listed between those stations.

As an added means of identification, each hydrologic station and partial-record station has been assigned a station number. These station numbers are in the same downstream order used in this report. In assigning a station number, no distinction is made between partial-record stations and other stations; therefore, the station number for a partial-record station indicates downstream-order position in a list composed of both types of stations. Gaps are consecutive. The complete 8-digit (or 10-digit) number for each station such as 09004100, which appears just to the left of the station name, includes a 2-digit part number "09" plus the 6-digit (or 8-digit) downstream order number "004100." In areas of high station density, an additional two digits may be added to the station identification number to yield a 10-digit number. The stations are numbered in downstream order as described above between stations of consecutive 8-digit numbers.

Evaluation of the Groundwater Flow Model for Southern Utah and Goshen Valleys, Utah, Updated to Conditions through 2011, with New Projections and Groundwater Management Simulations

By Lynette E. Brooks

Abstract

The U.S. Geological Survey (USGS), in cooperation with the Southern Utah Valley Municipal Water Association, updated an existing USGS model of southern Utah and Goshen Valleys for hydrologic and climatic conditions from 1991 to 2011 and used the model for projection and groundwater management simulations. All model files used in the transient model were updated to be compatible with MODFLOW-2005 and with the additional stress periods. The well and recharge files had the most extensive changes. Discharge to pumping wells in southern Utah and Goshen Valleys was estimated and simulated on an annual basis from 1991 to 2011. Recharge estimates for 1991 to 2011 were included in the updated model by using precipitation, streamflow, canal diversions, and irrigation groundwater withdrawals for each year. The model was evaluated to determine how well it simulates groundwater conditions during recent increased withdrawals and drought, and to determine if the model is adequate for use in future planning. In southern Utah Valley, the magnitude and direction of annual water-level fluctuation simulated by the updated model reasonably match measured water-level changes, but they do not simulate as much decline as was measured in some locations from 2000 to 2002. Both the rapid increase in groundwater withdrawals and the total groundwater withdrawals in southern Utah Valley during this period exceed the variations and magnitudes simulated during the 1949 to 1990 calibration period. It is possible that hydraulic properties may be locally incorrect or that changes, such as land use or irrigation diversions, occurred that are not simulated. In the northern part of Goshen Valley, simulated water-level changes reasonably match measured changes. Farther south, however, simulated declines are much less than measured declines. Land-use changes indicate that groundwater withdrawals in Goshen Valley are possibly greater than estimated and simulated. It is also possible that irrigation methods, amount of diversions, or other factors have changed that are not simulated or that aquifer properties are incorrectly simulated. The model can be used for projections about the effects of future groundwater withdrawals and managed aquifer recharge in southern Utah Valley, but rapid changes in withdrawals and increasing withdrawals dramatically may reduce the accuracy of the predicted water-level and groundwater-budget changes. The model should not be used for projections in Goshen Valley until additional withdrawal and discharge data are collected and the model is recalibrated if necessary. Model projections indicate large drawdowns of up to 400 feet and complete cessation of natural discharge in some areas with potential future increases in water use. Simulated managed aquifer recharge counteracts those effects. Groundwater management examples indicate that drawdown could be less, and discharge at selected springs could be greater, with optimized groundwater withdrawals and managed aquifer recharge than without optimization. Recalibration to more recent stresses and seasonal stress periods, and collection of new withdrawal, stream, land-use, and discharge data could improve the model fit to water-level changes and the accuracy of predictions.

Introduction

Groundwater is the primary source of drinking water in southern Utah Valley and the primary source of drinking water and irrigation water in Goshen Valley. Reported municipal and industrial withdrawals (Utah Division of Water Rights, 2012a) in southern Utah Valley doubled from 1999 to 2000, but did not continue increasing. The average amount of withdrawals from 2001 to 2011 was about the same as withdrawals in 2000. Increased withdrawals and below-average precipitation and streamflow from 2000 to 2003 caused water levels in many wells in the area to decline to their lowest recorded levels by 2005 (Burden and others, 2012, fig. 14). Water-level declines could affect the ability to withdraw water from wells, and could affect discharge to springs, drains, streams, flowing wells, and Utah Lake.

The U.S. Geological Survey (USGS), in cooperation with the Southern Utah Valley Municipal Water Association, updated an existing USGS model of southern Utah and Goshen Valleys (Brooks and Stolp, 1995) for hydrologic and climatic conditions from 1991 through 2011. The existing model simulated conditions from 1949 to 1990. Numerical models are constructed on the basis of available information and data; if new data become available, testing the model with those data will result in a better understanding of the model and the groundwater system (Konikow and Bredehoft, 1992). The model was evaluated to determine how well it simulates groundwater conditions during recent increased withdrawals and drought, and to determine if the model is adequate for use in future planning. Groundwater flow models can be used to help understand the effects of increased withdrawals, for analyses of managed aquifer recharge, or other scenarios. The model was used to simulate the effects of projected groundwater withdrawals and managed aquifer recharge through 2050 and to demonstrate uses of groundwater management simulations.

Purpose and Scope

This report evaluates an extended simulation period of a numerical model of the groundwater flow system in southern Utah and Goshen Valleys, Utah, that originally simulated conditions from 1949 to 1990 (Brooks and Stolp, 1995). Estimates of annual recharge to the system and discharge from wells from 1991 to 2011 were added to the model, and the model performance was evaluated. Land-use changes between 1991 and 2011 were not simulated in the model. This report also presents projection simulations that have increased withdrawals and managed aquifer recharge, and example groundwater management simulations to demonstrate the utility of optimization modeling for the period 2012 to 2050.

Description of Study Area

The study area covers about 390 mi^2 in southern Utah and Goshen Valleys in the north-central part of Utah and corresponds to the extent of the unconsolidated basin-fill deposits (fig.1). Utah Lake occupies much of the northern part of the study area and covers about 75 mi^2 of the study area. The study area is bounded by the Wasatch Range on the east and south, by the East Tintic Mountains on the west, and by an arbitrary divide on the north. The two valleys are separated by Utah Lake and West Mountain, but are hydraulically connected beneath Utah Lake and south of West Mountain.

Land-surface altitude in the study area, excluding West Mountain, ranges from 4,489 ft at Utah Lake to about 5,200 ft at the southeastern edge of Utah Valley. Altitudes in the Wasatch Range east of the study area exceed 10,000 ft, the highest altitude in the East Tintic Mountains west of the study area is about 6,400 ft, and the altitude of West Mountain is about 6,900 ft.

The population of incorporated areas of southern Utah Valley increased from about 47,000 to 112,000 from 1991 to 2011. Land is being converted from agricultural to urban and suburban use to accommodate this growth, and the locations and amounts of water use and applied water may be changing. The changes in land use and water use have the potential to affect groundwater levels; recharge; discharge to springs, drains, and streams; and water quality. To incorporate land-use changes in the numerical model and to evaluate the possible effects of land-use and associated water-use changes would have required additional data collection and a recalibration of the model, which were beyond the scope of this project.

Groundwater Hydrology

The groundwater system simulated by this model includes the upper 1,000 ft of basin-fill deposits in the valleys. At least one well has recently been completed in the consolidated rock in the southeast part of Utah Valley, but the basin fill is considered the principal aquifer in the study area. Lacustrine, alluvial, and colluvial processes deposited and sorted the basin-fill deposits according to the level of valley lakes and location of streams at the time of deposition (Brooks and Stolp, 1995, p. 13). These depositional environments create alternating and interfingering layers and lenses, causing vertical and horizontal heterogeneity in the basin fill.

Groundwater occurs in the basin-fill deposits under unconfined and confined conditions. Groundwater is unconfined in the poorly sorted deposits near the mountains, but becomes confined toward the center of the valleys as clay lenses become more prominent in the deposits (Brooks and Stolp, 1995, p. 15). Unconfined conditions exist in about the upper 50 ft of deposits throughout the two valleys. Both confined and unconfined water are considered to be part of the main groundwater system (fig. 2).

Recharge to the groundwater system is from subsurface inflow from consolidated rocks surrounding the valleys, streams and canals, irrigation, and precipitation on the valley (table 1). Groundwater discharge is to springs and drains, evapotranspiration, wells, streams and canals, Utah Lake, and sewer systems that act as drains in some locations.

The only part of the study area with a continuous clay layer is the Mapleton Bench, which is near the mountains between Hobble Creek and Spanish Fork River (fig. 1). The Mapleton Bench is underlain by at least one thick, continuous layer of clay, locally mixed with sand and silt (Brooks and Stolp, 1995, p. 15). The clay isolates the unconfined groundwater system in this area from the main groundwater system (Brooks and Stolp, 1995, fig. 6). Recharge from precipitation, irrigation, streams, and canals in this area becomes discharge to springs along the outer margins of the bench (Richardson, 1906, p. 53) and to Hobble Creek and Mill Race Canal (Brooks and Stolp, 1995, p. 31). The perched system on the Mapleton Bench is not included in the groundwater flow model; more detail about the groundwater budget in the Mapleton Bench area can be found in Brooks and Stolp (1995).

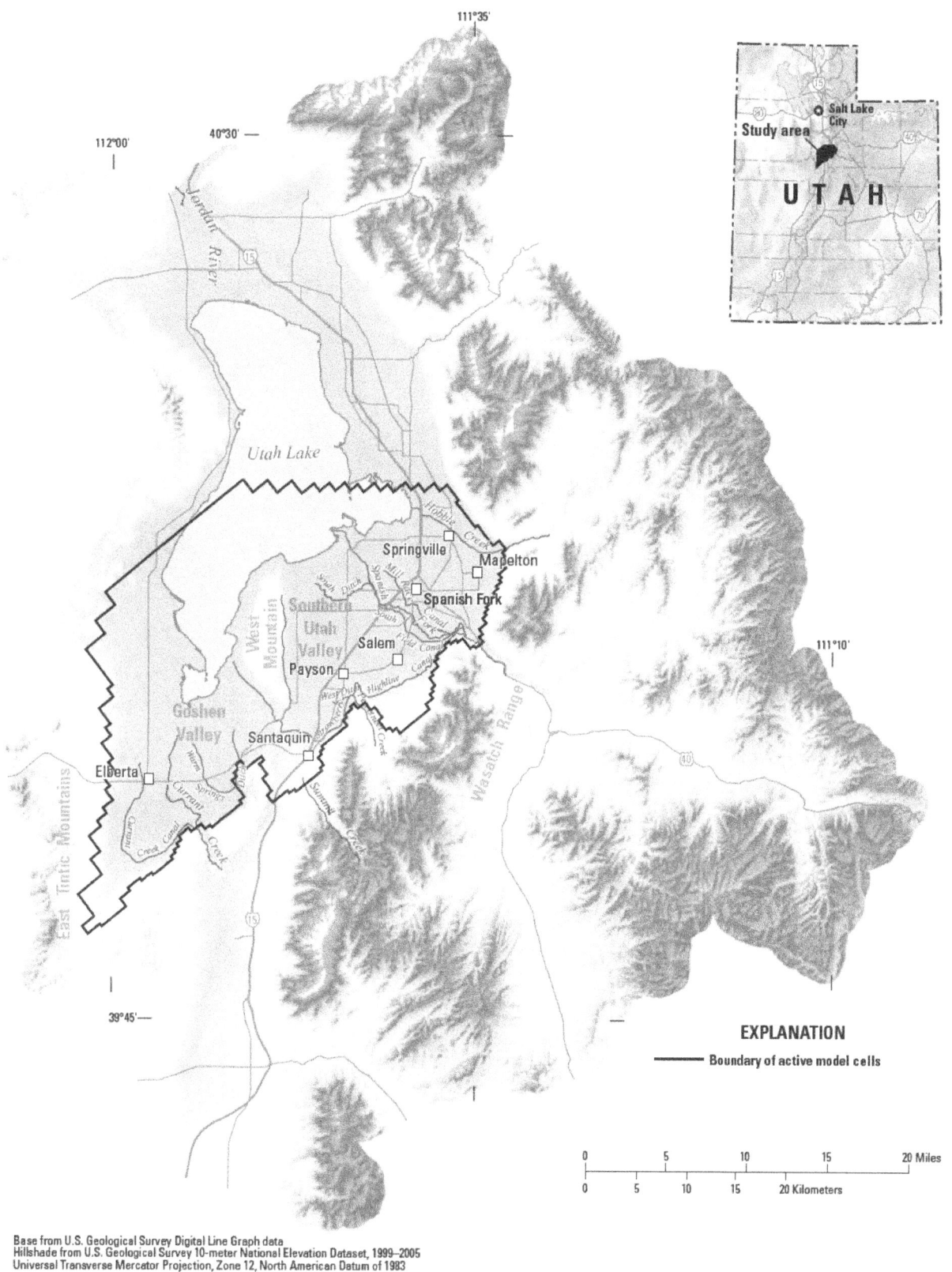

111°35'

112°00'

40°30' —

111°10'

39°45' —

Jordan River

Utah Lake

Hobble Creek

Springville

Mapelton

Spanish Fork

South Ditch

Spanish

Mill

Salem

Payson

West Mountain

Southern Utah Valley

Goshen Valley

Santaquin

Elberta

Warm Springs

Currant

Creek Canal

Creek

West Ditch Highline

Summit Creek

East Tintic Mountains

Wasatch Range

UTAH

Study area

Salt Lake City

EXPLANATION

———— Boundary of active model cells

0   5   10   15   20 Miles

0   5   10   15   20 Kilometers

Base from U.S. Geological Survey Digital Line Graph data
Hillshade from U.S. Geological Survey 10-meter National Elevation Dataset, 1999–2005
Universal Transverse Mercator Projection, Zone 12, North American Datum of 1983

Figure 1.   Location of southern Utah and Goshen Valleys study area, Utah.

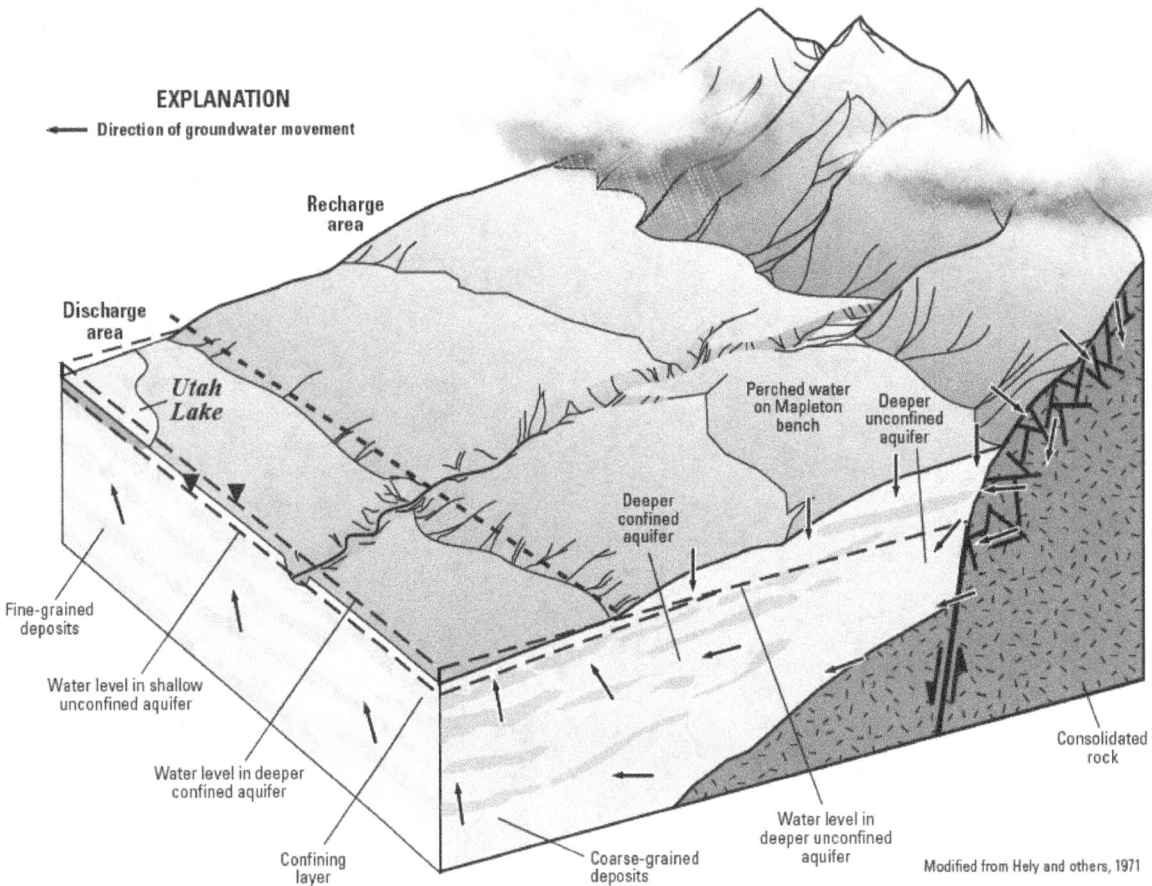

Figure 2.   Generalized block diagram showing the basin-fill groundwater system in southern Utah and Goshen Valleys, Utah.

Table 1.   Conceptual groundwater budget for the main groundwater system in the basin fill, southern Utah and Goshen Valleys, Utah, 1990.

[Modified from Brooks and Stolp, 1995, table 4 All flows in acre-feet per year —, not applicable]

Budget Element	Flow, in acre-feet			Budget Element	Flow, in acre-feet		
	Southern Utah Valley	Goshen Valley	Study area		Southern Utah Valley	Goshen Valley	Study area
Recharge				**Discharge**			
Subsurface inflow	[1] 65,000	[1] 13,000	[1,2] 79,000	Springs and drains	42,700	0	42,700
Perennial streams and major canals	33,400	8,100	41,500	Evapotranspiration	26,000	14,000	40,000
Irrigation and precipitation	14,900	400	15,300	Pumped wells	14,000	13,500	27,500
Intermittent and ephemeral runoff	6,400	400	6,800	Perennial streams and major canals	20,700	2,200	22,900
Intervalley flow[3]	0	7,800	—	Utah Lake	9,600	3,600	13,200
Total recharge (rounded)	120,000	30,000	[3] 143,000	Sewer systems	5,000	0	5,000
				Flowing wells	4,400	0	4,400
				Intervalley flow[3]	7,800	0	—
				Total discharge (rounded)	**130,000**	**33,000**	[3] **156,000**
				Water going into (+) or out of (-) storage[4] (rounded)	-9,800	-3,400	-13,200

[1] Calculated as a residual of the discharge minus all other forms of recharge

[2] Total for study area does not equal sum of two valleys because of rounding error

[3] Intervalley flow not used for study area total

[4] Water going into (+) storage is considered to be discharge and should be added to total discharge; water going out of (-) storage is considered to be recharge and should be added to total recharge

Description of the 1995 Southern Utah and Goshen Valleys Groundwater Flow Model

The USGS developed a numerical model in 1995 to simulate the groundwater system in the basin fill in southern Utah and Goshen Valleys (Brooks and Stolp, 1995). Model construction, discretization, recharge, discharge, and MODFLOW packages used are described in Brooks and Stolp (1995) and are summarized here. The model was constructed using the MODFLOW program (McDonald and Harbaugh, 1988) and consists of 45 rows, 103 columns, and 5 layers (fig. 3). Cell size ranges from 0.03 mi^2 to 0.9 mi^2 (Brooks and Stolp, 1995, p. 54). The model simulates recharge from consolidated rock, irrigation and precipitation on the basin fill, and streams and canals. The model simulates groundwater discharge to evapotranspiration, pumping wells, springs, drains, flowing wells, streams, Utah Lake, and sewer systems. Impermeable boundaries are assumed below 1,000 ft in the basin fill and at the contact between basin fill and consolidated rock at the edges of the valleys.

Recharge

The model simulates inflow from consolidated rock, recharge from mine-water dispersion ponds in Goshen Valley, irrigation and precipitation, and streams and canals. The model uses the Recharge Package (McDonald and Harbaugh, 1988, p. 7–1), the Well Package (McDonald and Harbaugh, 1988, p. 8–1), and the Stream Package (Prudic, 1989) to simulate these processes.

Inflow to both valleys from consolidated rock of the surrounding mountains was simulated with injection wells in model layers 1 and 2 along the boundary of the active cells. The location and amounts of inflow were determined during

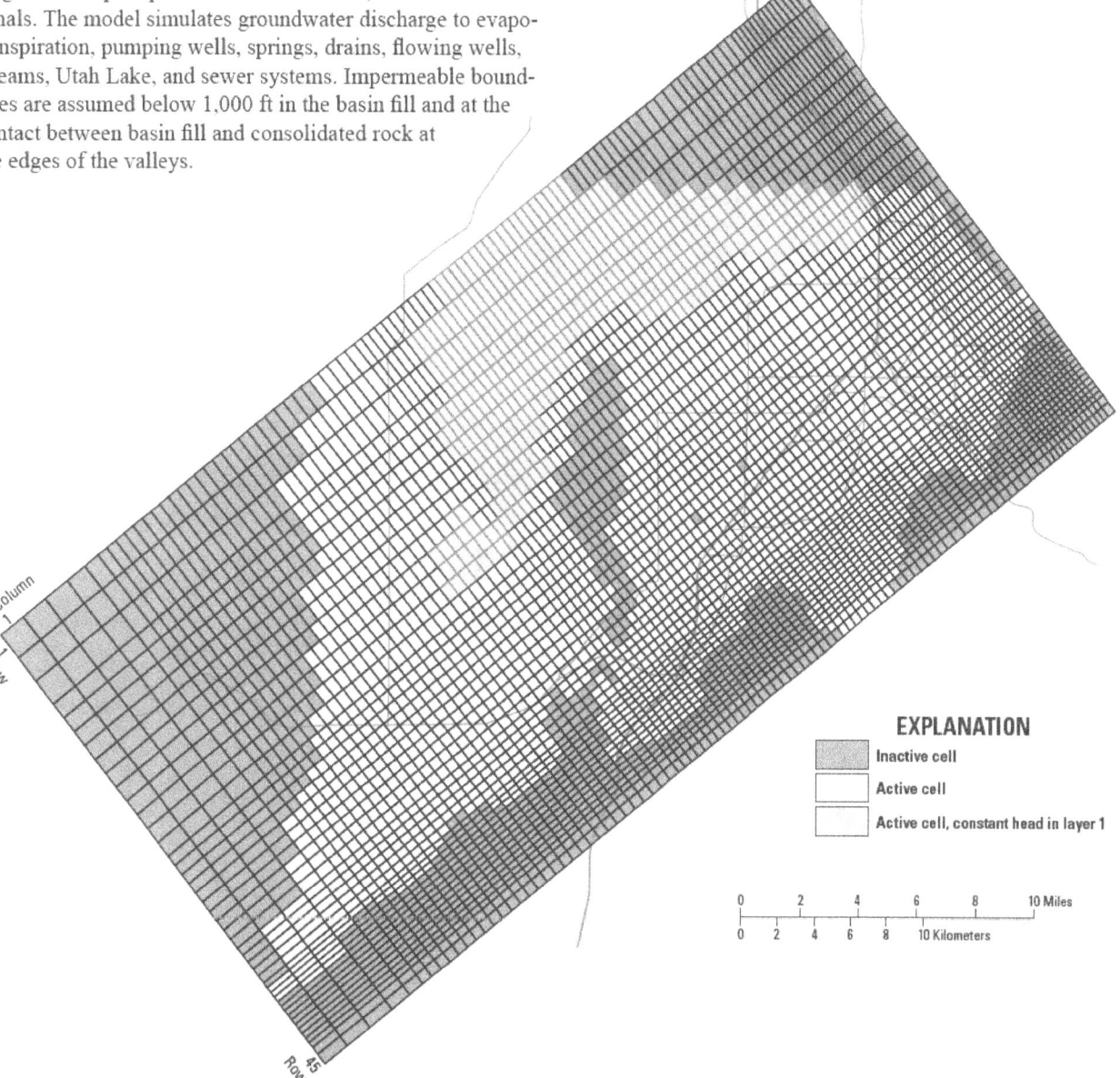

EXPLANATION

Inactive cell

Active cell

Active cell, constant head in layer 1

Figure 3. Numerical model grid, southern Utah and Goshen Valleys, Utah.

model calibration (Brooks and Stolp, 1995, p. 63). The amount of inflow from consolidated rock does not vary during the transient simulations. Mine water from the East Tintic Mountains was dispersed in ponds in Goshen Valley from 1969 to 1976; this is simulated with a single injection well in model layer 1.

Recharge from precipitation and irrigation is simulated as a specified-flux boundary by using the Recharge Package (McDonald and Harbaugh, 1988, p. 7–1) and applied to the highest active cell. Recharge from irrigation and precipitation on cropland is dependent on the amount of water applied, soil type, method of application, and crop type. Geographic information system (GIS) methods were used to divide the study area into zones representing these differences. Diversions from surface water were tabulated, and the amount of surface water and groundwater applied to each irrigation area was determined annually. Summer precipitation was included in the consumptive-use estimates, and winter precipitation (November through March) was considered to be applied water. Recharge in each area was calculated annually on the basis of equation 1 (Brooks and Stolp, 1995, table 6):

Recharge = [(applied surface water + applied groundwater + winter precipitation) × infiltration coefficient] - consumptive use   (1)

Recharge from precipitation on undeveloped land was assumed to be 10 percent of annual precipitation near the mountains in southern Utah Valley and 5 percent of annual precipitation in the middle of the valley in southern Utah Valley (Brooks and Stolp, 1995, fig. 8). Recharge from precipitation on undeveloped land in Goshen Valley is assumed to be negligible. Recharge from all sources simulated by using the Recharge Package is shown on figure 4.

Perennial streams and major canals are simulated by using the Stream Package (Prudic, 1989) if the amount of recharge or discharge was estimated to be dependent on the groundwater level near the stream or canal (fig. 5). Other perennial streams and canals were simulated by using the Recharge Package because the groundwater level is as much as 400 ft below the stream or canal (Brooks and Stolp, 1995, p. 57). Recharge from canals simulated with the Recharge Package was constant during the transient simulation; recharge from West Ditch, Summit Creek, and ephemeral streams varied annually on the basis of the natural flow in Spanish Fork River near Castilla (U.S. Geological Survey, 2012).

Discharge

Discharge from the groundwater system is simulated to springs, drains, evapotranspiration, streams, wells, Utah Lake, and sewer systems. These processes are simulated by the use of the Drain Package (McDonald and Harbaugh, 1988, p. 9–1), the Evapotranspiration Package (McDonald and Harbaugh, 1988, p. 10–1), the Stream Package, the Well Package, and the Time-Variant Specified Head (CHD) Package (Leake and Prudic, 1991, Appendix C). Except for pumped wells, all discharge is simulated as head-dependent boundaries (Brooks and Stolp, 1995, p. 63–64) and fluctuates in the transient model in response to changes in simulated water levels. Annual withdrawals for pumped irrigation, municipal, and industrial wells are simulated. Domestic wells and small flowing wells are not simulated.

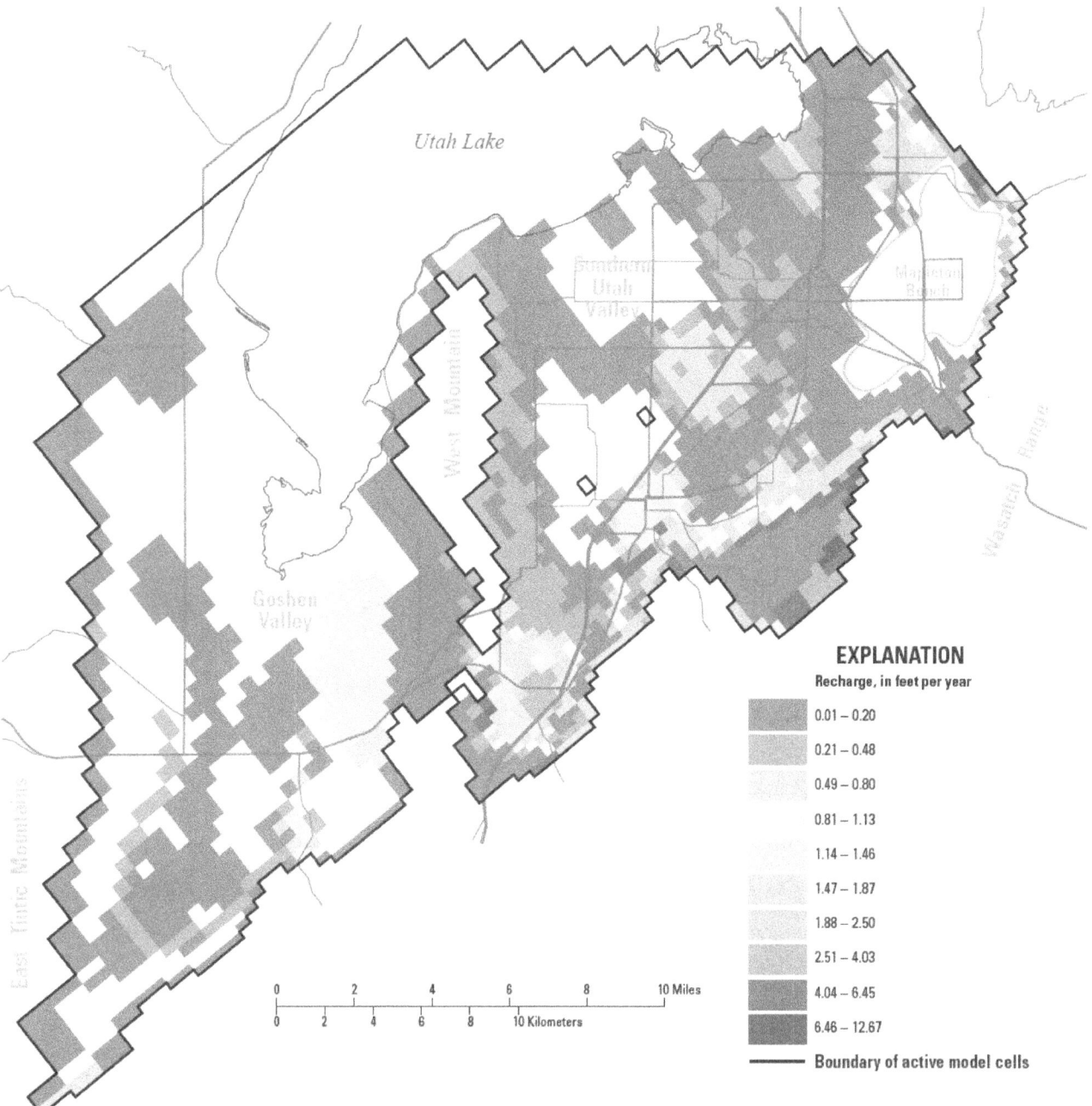

Figure 4.   Average recharge simulated using the Recharge Package in the numerical model from 1949 to 1990, southern Utah and Goshen Valleys, Utah.

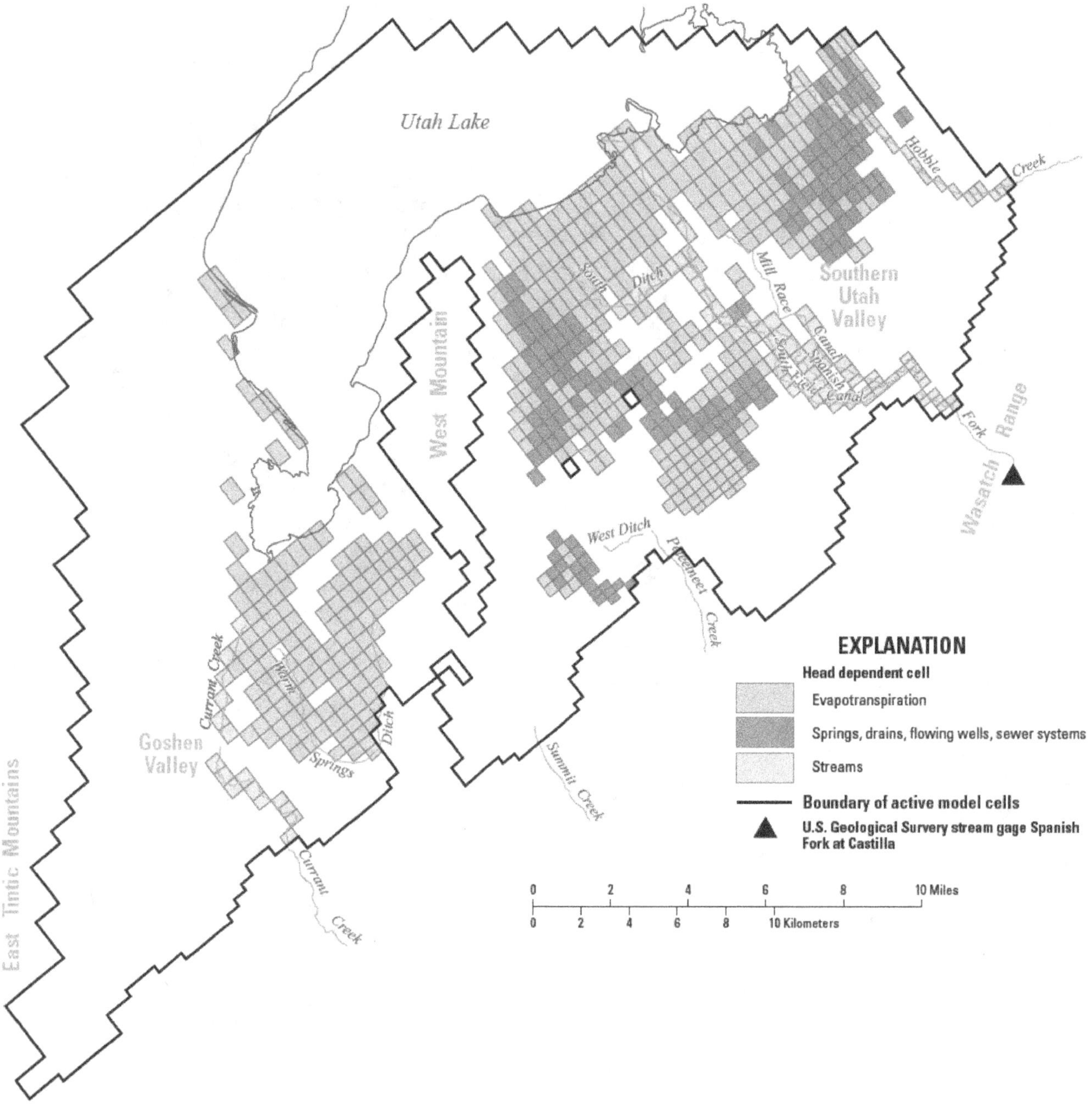

Figure 5.   Location of head-dependent boundaries in the numerical model, southern Utah and Goshen Valleys, Utah.

Update of the Model to Conditions Through 2011

The model files used in the transient model (Brooks and Stolp, 1995) were updated to be compatible with MOD-FLOW-2005 (Harbaugh, 2005). GIS methods were used during this process to ensure accurate spatial control of physical features and the finite-difference model grid. Model arrays were imported to the GIS model grid to enable visualization of aquifer properties, heads, drawdowns, and model features.

For the update period, the well and recharge files had the most extensive changes, and these changes are discussed in more detail in following sections. Minor changes were made to other files to enable the updated transient model to simulate 63 stress periods (1949 to 2011) instead of the original 42 stress periods (1949 to 1990). The altitude of Utah Lake was changed during the new stress periods on the basis of lake altitude or volume on March 15 of each year (Utah Division of Water Rights, 2012b); the lake level also varied annually in the original model (Brooks and Stolp, 1995, p. 64).

The average streamflow simulated from 1949 to 1990 was used for the new 21 stress periods in the Stream Package. In the original model, the discharge of selected streams was varied annually; this is no longer possible because data are not being collected for the two river systems (Spanish Fork River and Hobble Creek) that were simulated with varying flow rates in the original model. No flow data are being collected on the amount of water being diverted from Spanish Fork River to the Power Canal just to the east of the study area, or on how much water returns to the river downstream from the Power Canal. No flow data are being collected on Hobble Creek. An analysis of flow rates and associated simulated gains

and losses in the rivers (table 2) in the original model indicates little difference in the net recharge with flow in Hobble Creek, and an inverse difference in the net recharge with flow in Spanish Fork River. Higher flows in Spanish Fork River appear to be associated with higher water levels and more discharge to the river; the amount of flow in the river may have little influence on the amount of recharge and discharge. Holding these stresses constant during the updated model period is not expected to have a significant effect on model performance. The exception would be if decreased water levels cause enough stream loss to deplete the streams during periods of low flow, but data are not available for this analysis.

Hydraulic properties of the groundwater system were not changed. The distribution and amount of inflow from consolidated rock simulated by using the Well Package were kept constant throughout the 63 stress periods as they were in the original model. The distribution and properties of head-dependent boundaries to simulate discharge to evapotranspiration, springs, drains, flowing wells, and sewer systems were kept constant throughout the 63 stress periods. The recharge or discharge at head-dependent boundaries changes during the original and extended transient model in response to changes in simulated water levels.

Groundwater Withdrawals

Discharge to pumping wells in southern Utah and Goshen Valleys was estimated and simulated on an annual basis from 1991 to 2011. Annual withdrawals from irrigation wells were estimated from unpublished data in the files of the U.S. Geological Survey Utah Water Science Center office in Salt Lake City, Utah. Annual withdrawals from municipal and industrial wells were obtained from the Utah Division of Water Rights (2012a). Annual withdrawals from 1991 to 1999 were of similar magnitude to previous years, with some fluctuation for climatic variation (fig. 6). Reported municipal withdrawals increased dramatically from 6,300 acre-ft in 1999 to 13,800 acre-ft in 2000. Since 2000, withdrawals have remained at the higher levels, but have not increased other than fluctuation for climatic variation. New wells (since 1990) are concentrated in the Spanish Fork and Springville area, the Santaquin area, and central Goshen Valley (fig. 7). The increase in municipal withdrawals from 1999 to 2000 is significant and was examined in more detail. A corresponding drop in water levels in a number of wells was also observed in the 1999 to 2004 period, which provides corroborative evidence for this sizeable increase in withdrawals. The likely explanation for this large year-to-year increase is a unique combination of climate effects on available spring discharge, increased growth in municipal demands, and the need for groundwater supplies to meet these demands. It is also possible that water use was under-reported in 1999 and that the increase was more gradual than appears by reported numbers.

Table 2. Comparison of simulated stream-aquifer interactions for varying flow rates in the original model, southern Utah Valley, Utah.

[Modified from Brooks and Stolp, 1995, table 18 All flows in acre-feet per year]

Year	1990	1964	1949	1983
Hobble Creek				
Starting flow	9,200	15,000	26,000	84,000
Recharge from stream	4,400	4,800	5,000	5,700
Discharge to stream	1,200	1,700	2,200	2,900
Net recharge	3,200	3,100	2,800	2,800
Spanish Fork River				
Starting flow	15,000	25,000	26,000	147,000
Recharge from stream	10,300	8,100	6,400	4,600
Discharge to stream	2,600	2,900	4,700	5,000
Net recharge	7,700	5,200	1,700	-400

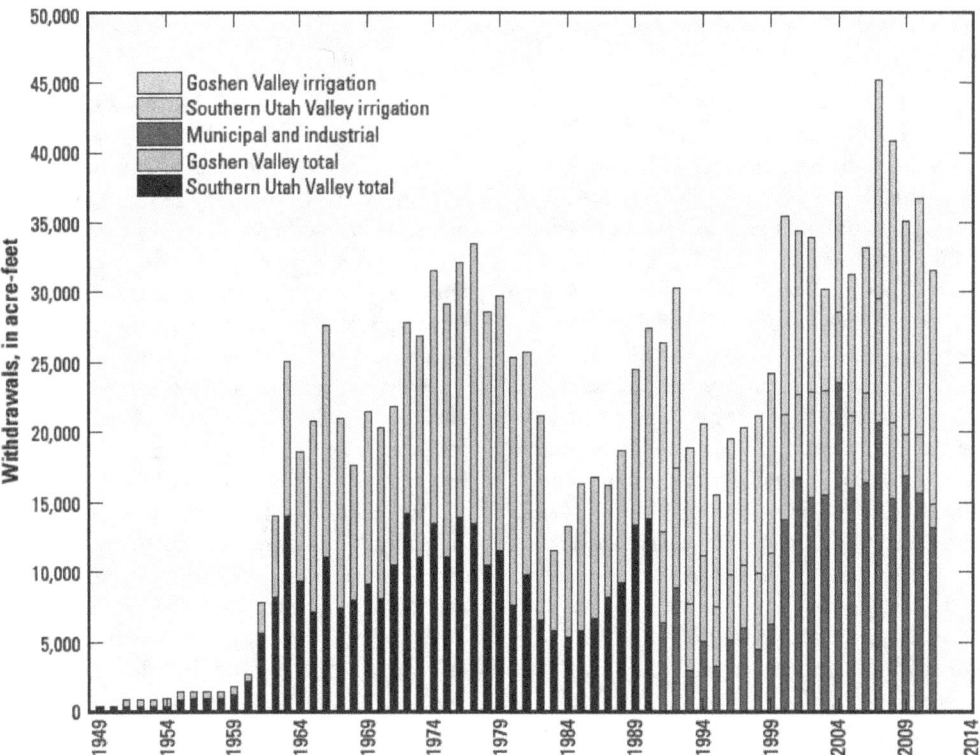

Figure 6.   Irrigation, municipal, and industrial groundwater withdrawals from 1949 to 2011, southern Utah and Goshen Valleys, Utah.

Recharge

Recharge estimates for 1991 to 2011 were developed using methods described by Brooks and Stolp (1995) by using precipitation, streamflow, canal diversions, and irrigation groundwater withdrawals for each year. Recharge from irrigation was determined by using equation 1, but minor changes were made from the previous estimates. First, the previous study changed consumptive use of each crop type on an annual basis. The update does not account for this because the small variation in annual consumptive use is negligible compared to unknown changes in land use, crop type, and irrigation method. The previously determined average annual consumptive use from 1949 to 1990 for each crop type in each valley was used for 1991 to 2011. Second, precipitation at Payson (Western Regional Climate Center, 2012a) was previously used, but that station has no data after June 1999. For this report, the precipitation at Payson is used through 1998 (with the exception of 1996, which is missing some data) and the precipitation at the Santaquin chlorinator (Western Regional Climate Center, 2012b) is used for 1996 and 1999 to 2011. During the period when data are available for both stations, Payson had an average April–March precipitation that was 0.94 times the April–March precipitation at the Santaquin chlorinator and an average November–March precipitation that was 1.03 times the precipitation at the Santaquin chlorinator. For consistency with the previous report and model, precipitation from the Santaquin chlorinator is multiplied by 1.03 for use in equation

1 and by 0.94 to estimate precipitation on the undeveloped areas.

Additional data needed to estimate recharge from irrigation included estimating annual applied surface water for select irrigated areas (table 3), average applied surface water for select irrigated areas, assignment of average municipal water applied to irrigated areas (including lawns and gardens), and assignment of groundwater withdrawals applied to irrigated areas. All areas with variable applied surface water received water from canals reported by the Spanish Fork River Commissioner (Utah Division of Water Rights, 2012b).

Recharge from West Ditch, Summit Creek, and ephemeral streams was varied during the updated stress periods on the basis of annual "natural" flow in the Spanish River at Castilla (USGS gaging station 10150500). The amount of water delivered from Strawberry Reservoir to the Spanish Fork River (John Mendenhall, Spanish Fork River Commissioner, written commun., August 2012) was subtracted from the gaged flow at Castilla (U.S. Geological Survey, 2012) for each year to determine the natural flow in the river. The original model varied these sources of recharge by the use of a multiplier of the 1949–90 average annual natural flow (Brooks and Stolp, 1995, fig. 7), but values were not reported by Brooks and Stolp (1995) for the 1949–90 average natural flow or for the 1990 natural flow. Brooks and Stolp (1995, p. 11) state that in 1990, natural flow in Spanish Fork at Castilla was 48 percent of the 1949–90 average annual flow. Calculations using data from U.S Geological Survey (2012) and John Mendenhall

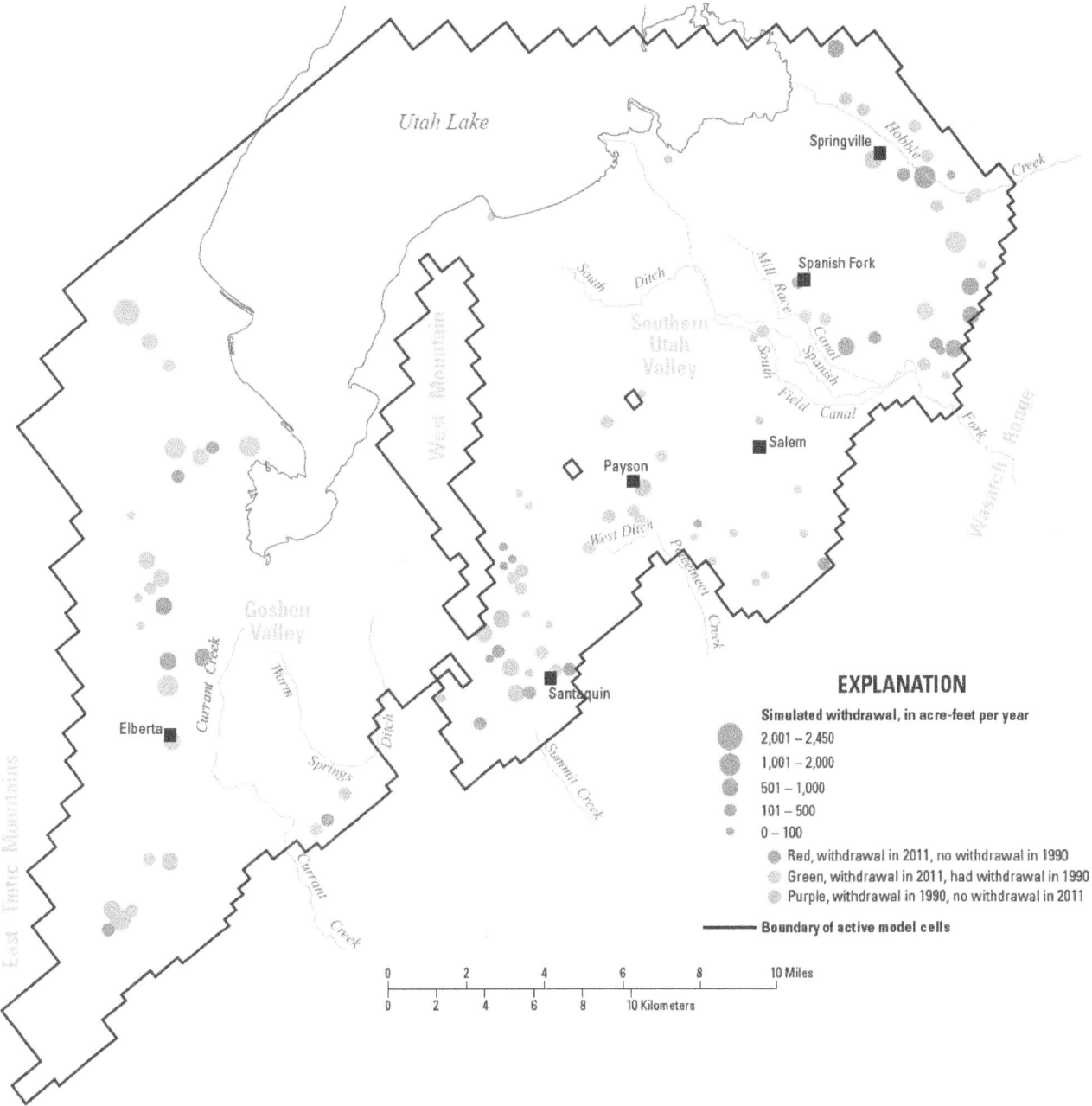

Figure 7. Location and magnitude of groundwater withdrawals in the numerical model, southern Utah and Goshen Valleys, Utah.

(Spanish Fork River Commissioner, written commun., August 2012) yield a value of natural flow in 1990 of 47,400 acre-feet. The 1949–90 average was calculated on the basis of calendar year annual flow to be 47,400 divided by 0.48, or about 98,800 acre-feet. This value was used as the average annual flow to determine the multiplier for West Ditch, Summit Creek, and ephemeral streams for each year from 1991 to 2011 in the updated model periods. The ratio of annual flow to average annual flow in the updated stress periods ranges from 0.38 in 1994 to 2.46 in 2011. Using these multipliers indicated that

the natural flow in the Spanish Fork River, and recharge from West Ditch, Summit Creek, and ephemeral streams, averaged about 25 percent more during 1991 to 2011 than during 1949 to 1990. This is consistent with precipitation at Spanish Fork Power House being greater in the more recent years (Burden and others, 2012, fig. 14). Average annual recharge simulated from all sources during the updated stress periods is similar to, but less variable than, average annual recharge simulated during the original transient simulation (fig. 8).

Table 3. Description of water applied to irrigated areas, southern Utah and Goshen Valleys, Utah.

[Applied surface water, listed as "variable", "none", or nonvariable amount, in acre-feet per year; applied groundwater, listed as "variable", "none", or nonvariable amount, in acre-feet per year]

Number of irrigated area[1]	Unofficial name of irrigated area	Applied surface water	Applied groundwater	Applied spring water, in acre-feet per year
Southern Utah Valley				
1	Springville City	4,460	none	481
3	Springville High-line	1,908	none	0
5	Sage	660	none	172
6	Swenson	2,447	variable	0
7	Dry Creek	none	variable	4,700
10	Westfield	variable	variable	0
11	Mill Race	2,400	none	0
12	Lake Shore	variable	none	0
13	Spanish Fork City	variable	[2] 1,600	0
14	South Field	variable	none	0
15	Salem	variable	variable	0
16	Salem City	1,000	[2] 320	0
17	Strawberry-One	variable	variable	0
18	Strawberry-Two	variable	variable	60
19	Strawberry-Three	variable	variable	170
20	Payson City	3,084	[2] 1,650	0
21	Summit	variable	variable	0
Goshen Valley				
22	Strawberry-Four	variable	none	0
23	Bateman-Howlett	none	variable	0
24	LDS North	none	variable	0
25	LDS Central	none	variable	0
26	LDS Orchards	none	variable	0
27	Goshen	7,153	none	0
29	Goshen Mouth	1,400	none	0
29	Currant	[3] 6,390	variable	0
30	Lunceford-Ekin	none	variable	0

[1] Number refers to Brooks and Stolp (1995, table 6 and figure 8) Areas that recharge only the Mapleton Bench are not included

[2] Municipal supply used for irrigation

[3] Was variable in transient model, but flow records were not found for 1991–2011 Unpublished U S Geological Survey files indicate this amount was commonly used in original model

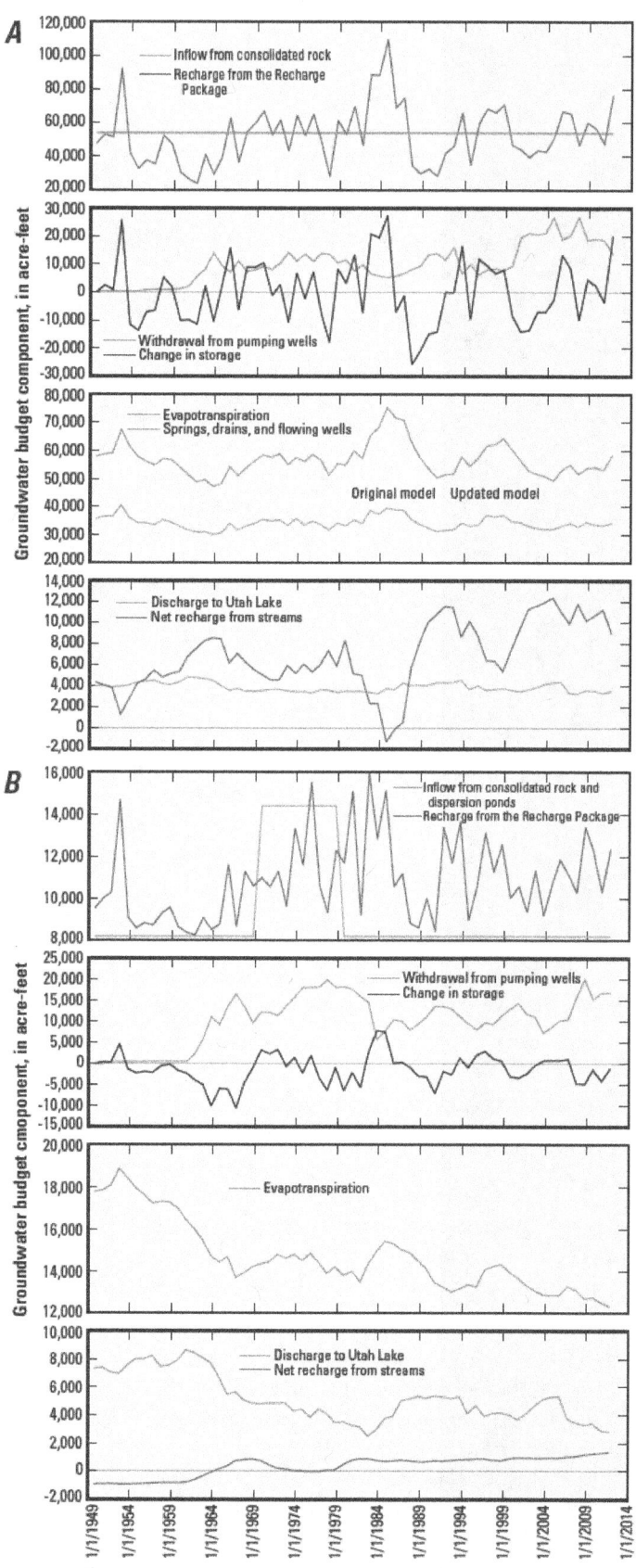

Figure 8. Simulated groundwater budget components for *A*, southern Utah Valley and *B*, Goshen Valley, Utah.

Performance of the Updated Model

The ability of the updated transient model to match hydrologic conditions determined for 1991 to 2011 was evaluated by comparing water-level changes measured in wells to changes simulated by the model. The match or mismatch of levels before 1991 was evaluated as part of model calibration in Brooks and Stolp (1995) and was not considered a factor in this evaluation of the ability of the model to simulate more recent conditions. Model performance was not evaluated for changes in natural discharges because few observations were available from 1991 to 2011. Water-level measurements made in March of multiple years between 1991 and 2012 exist for 18 wells in southern Utah Valley and 13 wells in Goshen Valley (fig. 9). March measurements collected throughout Utah are generally considered to represent the effects of the previous year's hydrologic conditions on the groundwater system and are used to examine long-term trends. The main recharge in April–June and the increased withdrawals from May–September of the previous year have the least local effect in March.

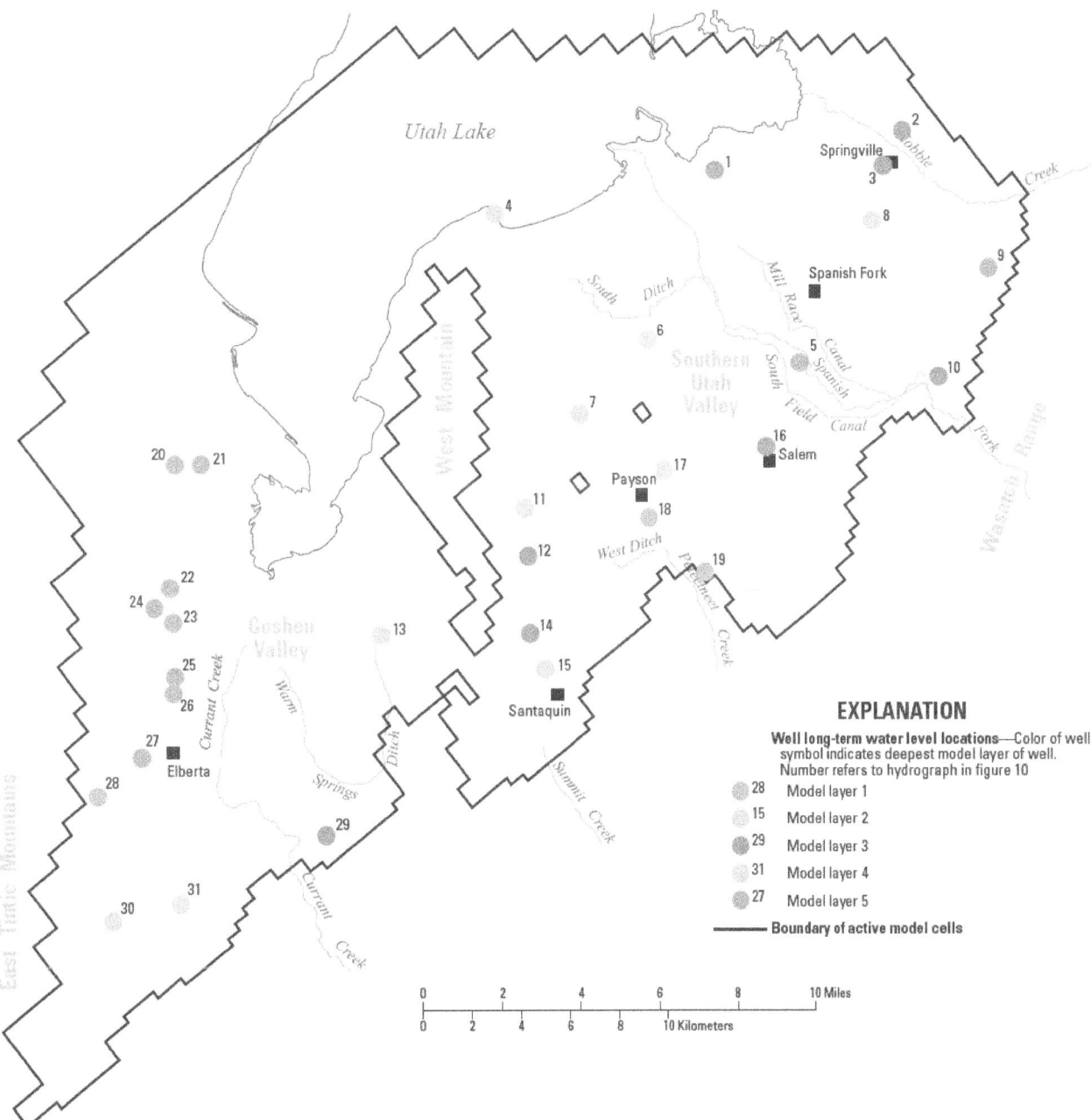

Figure 9.   Location and model layer of groundwater-level measurements, southern Utah and Goshen Valleys, Utah.

In southern Utah Valley, the magnitude and direction of annual water-level fluctuation simulated by the model reasonably match measured water-level changes (hydrographs 1–10 and 14–19 on fig. 10). The similar response indicates that the variation in annual recharge and annual withdrawals simulated in the model are generally good approximations of the actual changes in the groundwater system. The similar response also indicates that land-use changes have not had a major influence on groundwater recharge and that the hydraulic properties simulated in the model are appropriate. Measured and simulated water levels generally rise from the end of the original transient simulated period to about 1999, decline from 1999 to about 2005, and rise again after 2005. Although the hydrographs indicate a reasonable fit, an analysis of model fit to the water level in 25 wells measured in multiple years (table 4) indicates that the model does not match those levels as well as it matched 1991 levels. In Goshen Valley, simulated water levels do not decline as much as observed levels from 1991 to 2012. In southern Utah Valley, simulated water levels rise more from 1991 to 1999 than observed levels, but then more closely match the overall decline from 1999 to 2005 and the overall rise from 2005 to 2012.

In several areas, however, the model does not simulate as much decline as was measured from 2000 to 2002 (hydrographs 3, 5, 9, 12, 13, and 16 on fig. 10). The steep measured water-level declines in southern Utah Valley were probably the result of a rapid increase in withdrawals combined with below-average recharge (fig. 8*A*). Recharge from irrigation and precipitation during the early 2000s was below average, but was not as low as during other periods. The increase in municipal well withdrawals from 1999 to 2000 in southern Utah Valley, however, was unprecedented (fig. 6). In

the model, the simulated increase in withdrawals results in decrease in storage, decrease in discharge to evapotranspiration, decrease in discharge to drains (springs, drains, and flowing wells), and increase in recharge from streams (fig. 8). In the groundwater system, observed water-level changes indicate that the decrease in storage is greater than in the model (observed water-level declines are greater than simulated water-level declines). It is possible that increased recharge from streams or decreased discharge to evapotranspiration, springs, drains, and flowing wells may be less in the groundwater system than in the model; measurements are not available to examine the possible changes in the groundwater budget. Both the rapid increase in withdrawals and the total withdrawals in southern Utah Valley exceed changes and amounts that were simulated for the pre-1991 calibration period; it is possible that simulated hydraulic properties may be locally incorrect resulting in simulated changes in natural discharge that are faster than occur in the groundwater system. It is also possible that other changes in the system that are not simulated contributed to the steep groundwater-level decline; these could include difference in streamflow, differences in land use and irrigation, or other causes. The model reasonably simulates water-level changes after 2002, indicating that the rapid increase in withdrawals, not the amount of withdrawals, may be causing the discrepancy between the simulated water-level changes and the measured changes.

In the northern part of Goshen Valley, simulated water-level changes reasonably match measured changes (hydrographs 20–22 on fig. 10). Farther south, however, simulated declines are much less than measured declines (hydrographs 23–28 and 30 on fig. 10), even though in the transient calibration period, simulated changes reasonably matched measured changes. The pattern of measured declines in Goshen Valley indicates that groundwater withdrawals exceed recharge and the ability of the groundwater system to reduce natural discharge, so water withdrawn from wells is continuing to decrease storage in the groundwater system. The simulated water levels indicates that groundwater withdrawals are better balanced with recharge and the reduction in natural discharge, so less change in storage occurs. Land-use changes indicate that more land is being irrigated than during the previous study, but withdrawal records indicate similar amounts of groundwater were withdrawn recently and in the 1970s. It is possible that groundwater withdrawals in Goshen Valley are greater than simulated. It is also possible that unknown changes in recharge from Currant Creek, Currant Creek Canal, and the irrigation from Warm Springs have occurred that are not simulated. As a test of the possibility of less recharge, recharge from Currant Creek Canal and the Warm Springs distribution system was reduced in some simulations; simulated drawdowns increased only slightly. It is also possible that groundwater withdrawal during the calibration period did not cause enough stress to determine accurate hydraulic properties of the aquifer and that they are not simulated correctly.

Table 4. Summary statistics of model fit to 25 water-level observations, southern Utah and Goshen Valleys, Utah.
[All water levels in feet]

Year	Average observed value	Average simulated value	Average residual	Sum of squared residuals
Southern Utah Valley				
1991	4,598	4,605	-6	1,512
1999	4,605	4,615	-10	2,244
2000	4,603	4,613	-10	2,434
2002	4,595	4,607	-12	2,851
2005	4,592	4,603	-11	3,313
2012	4,601	4,611	-10	2,503
Goshen Valley				
1991	4,524	4,529	-4	822
1999	4,516	4,528	-12	2,513
2000	4,514	4,526	-12	2,239
2002	4,511	4,526	-15	2,610
2005	4,511	4,528	-17	7,811
2012	4,497	4,518	-21	6,666

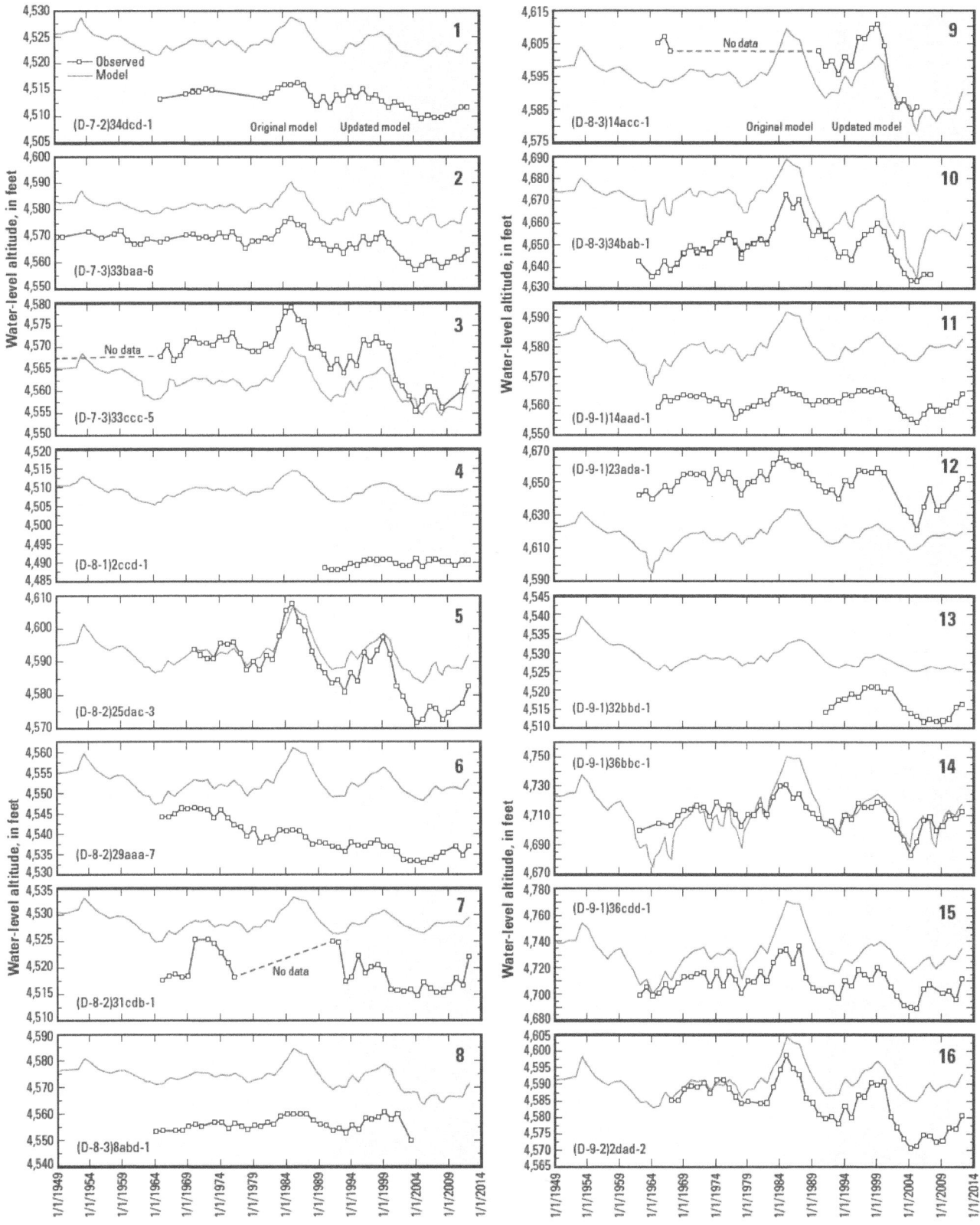

Figure 10.   Measured and simulated water levels, 1949 to 2012, southern Utah and Goshen Valleys, Utah.

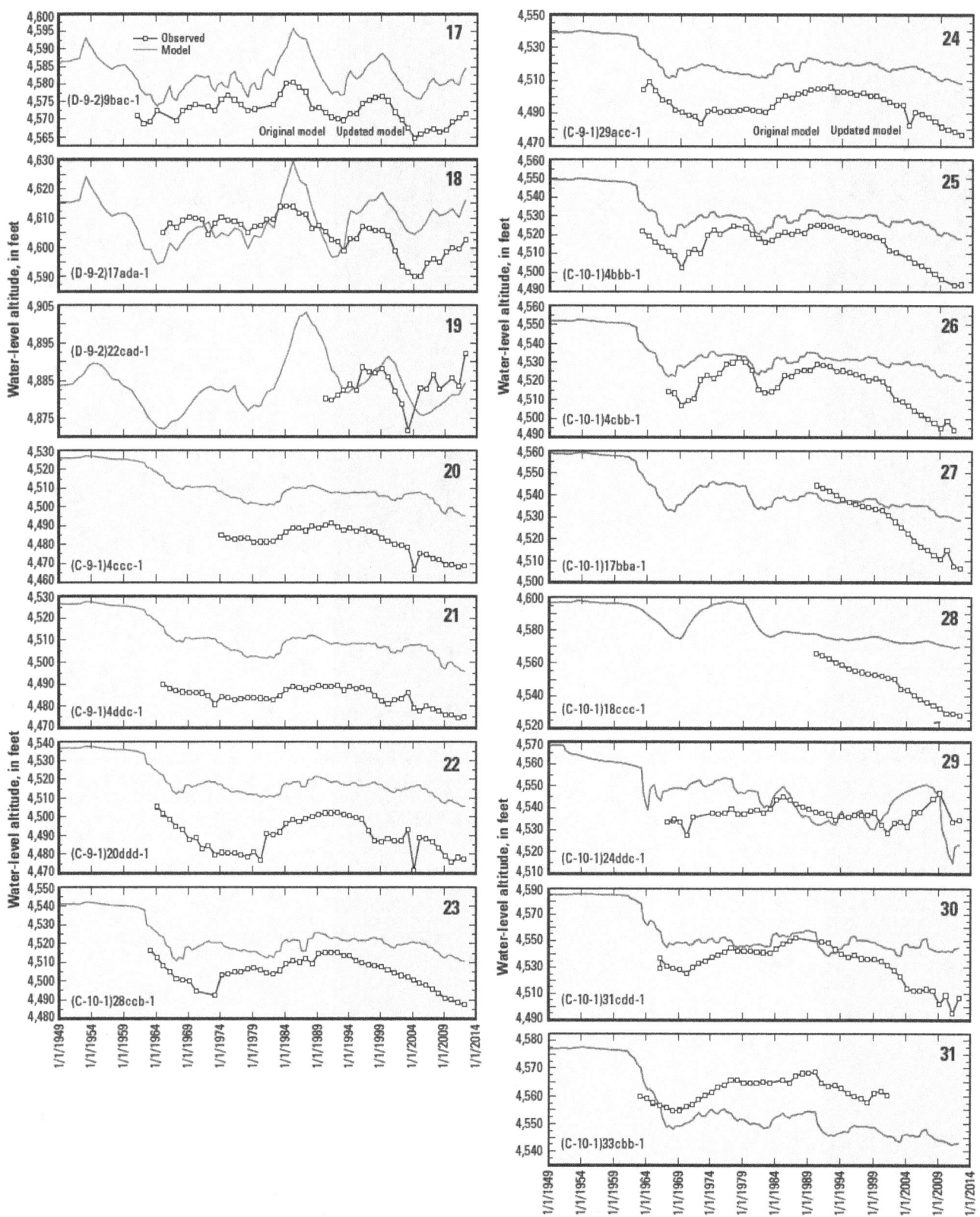

Figure 10. Measured and simulated water levels, 1949 to 2012, southern Utah and Goshen Valleys, Utah.—Continued

Appropriate Uses of the Model

Because the updated model reasonably represents conditions in southern Utah Valley, the model can be used for projection and groundwater management simulations of future groundwater withdrawals and managed aquifer recharge. Rapid changes in the system in response to greatly increased withdrawals may not be simulated correctly, and increasing withdrawals greatly over withdrawals simulated during the calibration period may reduce the accuracy of the projections. The model can also be used for particle tracking in southern Utah Valley to identify the source of water to wells and the possible flowpaths of recharged water if water-quality issues are identified. The model should not be used for projections in Goshen Valley until additional withdrawal and discharge data are collected and the model is recalibrated, if necessary, to improve the match of simulated water-level fluctuations to observed water-level fluctuations.

Model Projections 2012 to 2050

The updated groundwater model was used to estimate possible effects on the groundwater system and groundwater levels caused by increased groundwater withdrawals, changing the Strawberry Highline Canal from an unlined canal to a piped system, and the addition of managed aquifer recharge (MAR). One-year stress periods were used to simulate the following stress conditions: (1) average recharge and the same withdrawals as in 2010 projected from 2012 to 2050, (2) average recharge and increasing municipal withdrawals through 2050, (3) the same stresses as in (2) and assuming the

Strawberry Highline Canal is piped and does not recharge the groundwater system, and (4) the same stresses as in (3) with 30,000 acre-ft/yr of MAR.

Average recharge was determined by using the 2010 applied surface-water and groundwater amounts, a multiplier of 1.09 for recharge from ephemeral streams based on natural flow in the Spanish Fork River from 1949 to 2011, and multipliers for winter precipitation and total precipitation at Payson that represent the average from 1949 to 2011. Precipitation was used to calculate recharge as explained in the "Recharge" sections of this report. For the projections with increased withdrawals, municipal withdrawals were increased a total of about 55,000 acre-ft/yr by 2050 (Mark Chandler; Caldwell, Richards, and Sorensen (CRS) Engineers, written commun., October 3, 2012); earlier withdrawals are less (fig. 11). MAR was applied at locations and in amounts provided by Mark Chandler (CRS Engineers, written commun., March 8, 2012). The availability of water and land for recharge and the capability of infiltration in these areas (fig. 12) have not been verified by the USGS. Both the completion of piping of the Strawberry Highline Canal and the beginning of MAR were simulated to occur starting in the stress period representing 2017 in the projections.

Because of uncertainty in the accuracy of the updated model in Goshen Valley and because increased withdrawals are simulated mainly in southern Utah Valley, the effects of the projected changes on the simulated groundwater budget were analyzed only for southern Utah Valley, and projected simulated water-level hydrographs are presented only for southern Utah Valley. With average recharge and 2010 withdrawal rates (projection 1), the system reaches a new steady-state condition in about 10 years with minimal water-level declines and minimal changes to natural discharge or recharge from streams

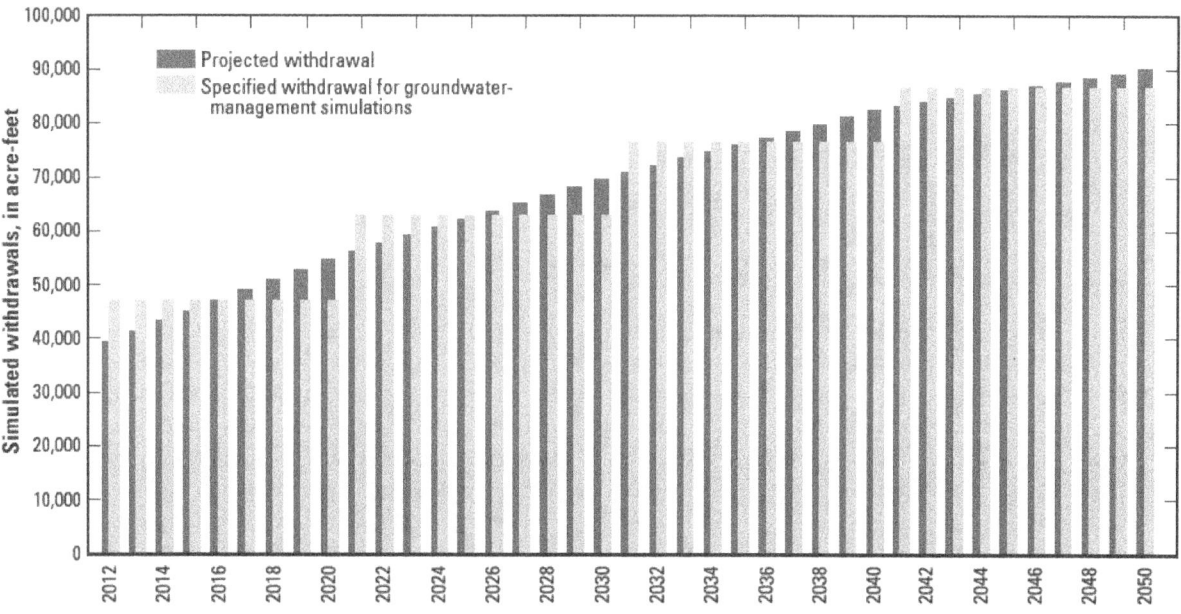

Figure 11.   Withdrawals simulated in projections 2, 3, and 4, and in groundwater management example 1, 2012 to 2050, southern Utah and Goshen Valleys, Utah.

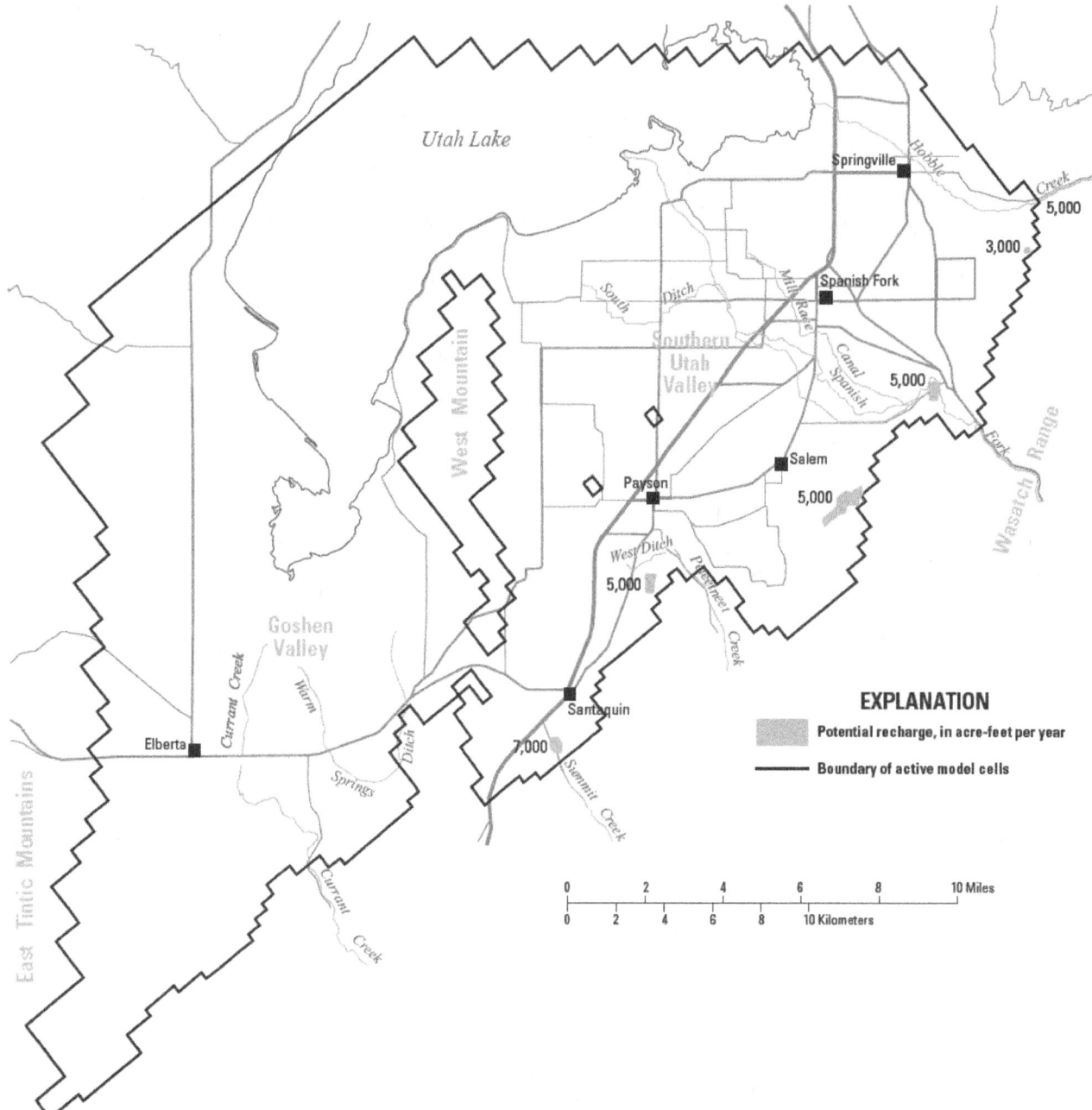

Figure 12.   Areas and amounts of projected managed aquifer recharge, southern Utah Valley, Utah.

(figs. 13 and 14). This projection provides the comparison for the next projections and is referred to as the base projection; drawdown is considered to be the simulated water level at the end of projection 1 minus the simulated water level at the end of projections 2, 3, and 4. The effects of projection 2 were only slightly less than the effects of projection 3 and are not shown on all the figures.

For the three projections with increased withdrawals, the maximum drawdown is about 400 ft (fig. 15), and in projection 3, some areas of natural discharge no longer discharge groundwater (fig. 14). Because withdrawals continue to increase, drawdown must continue outward until further

natural discharge is captured, and a new steady-state condition is not achieved by 2050; water levels continue to decline, natural discharge continues to decline, and recharge from streams continues to increase (figs. 13 and 14). A fifth projection continued the stresses at the end of projection 3 for another 50 years. Steady-state conditions were achieved within 10 years of withdrawals being held steady at the projected 2050 rates. The effects of the fifth projection are similar to the effects of projection 3 and are not shown on the figures. Projection 4, with MAR, reduces the effects of increased withdrawals and has less area with large water-level declines and less reduction in natural discharge than projection 3 (figs. 14 and 15).

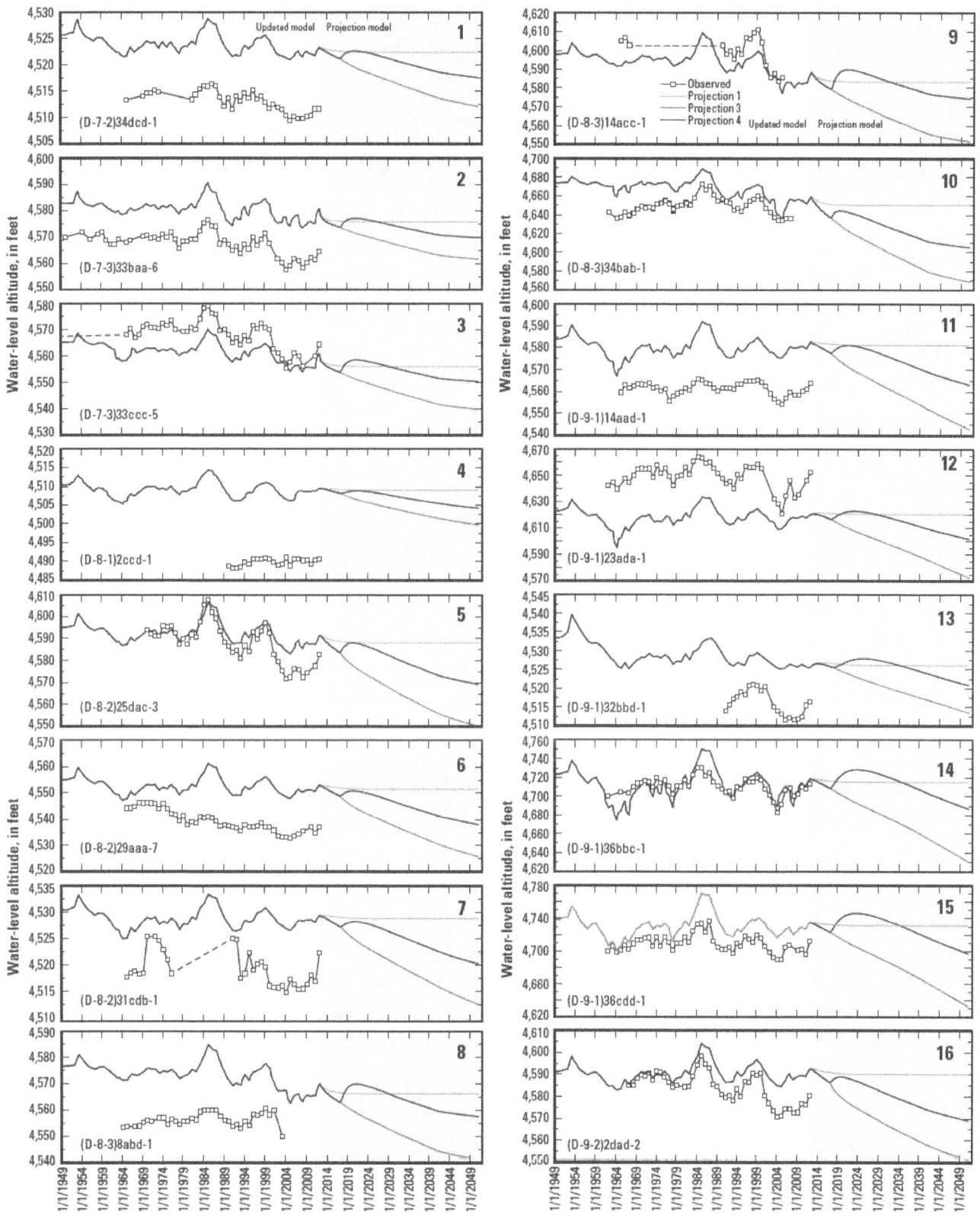

Figure 13.   Projected simulated water-level altitude in selected wells, southern Utah Valley, Utah.

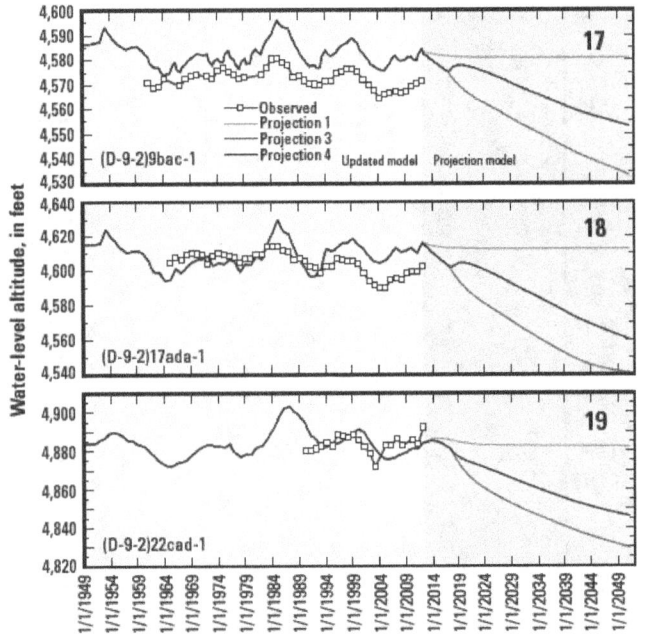

Figure 13. Projected simulated water-level altitude in selected wells, southern Utah Valley, Utah.—Continued

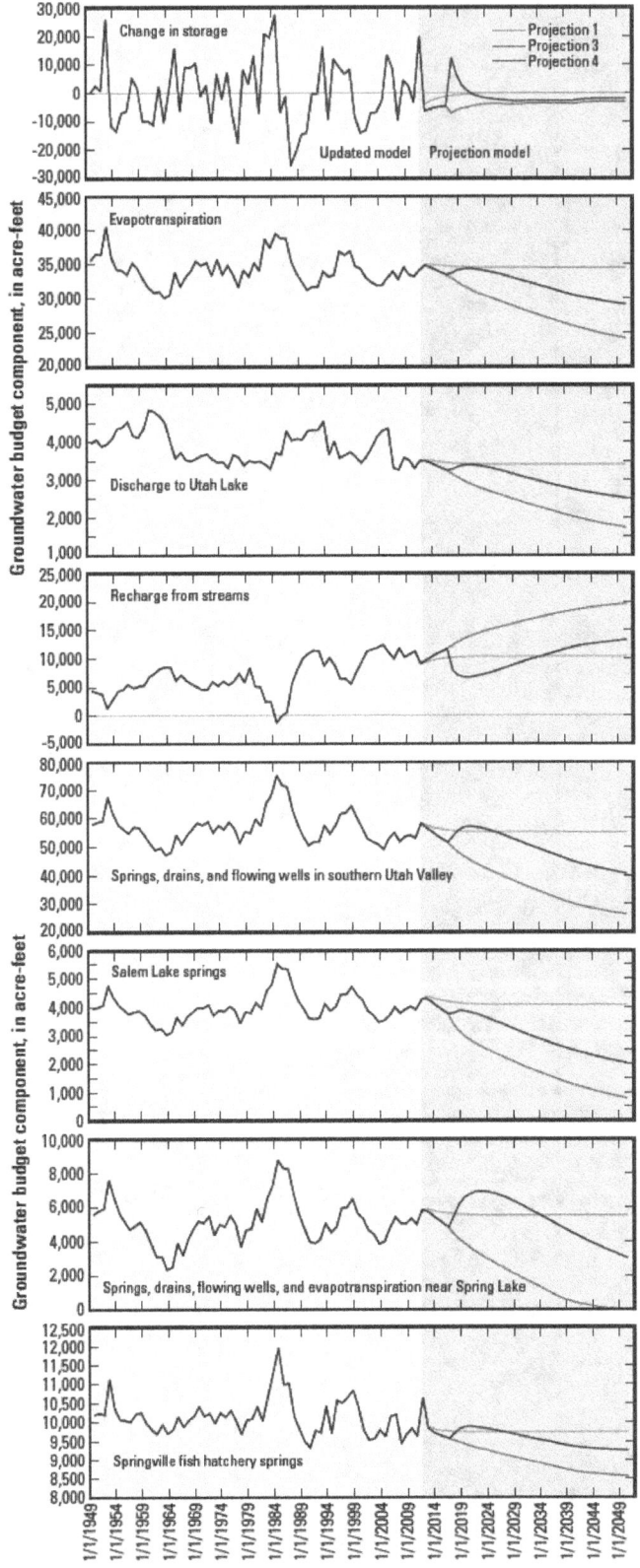

Figure 14. Projected simulated selected groundwater-budget components, southern Utah Valley, Utah.

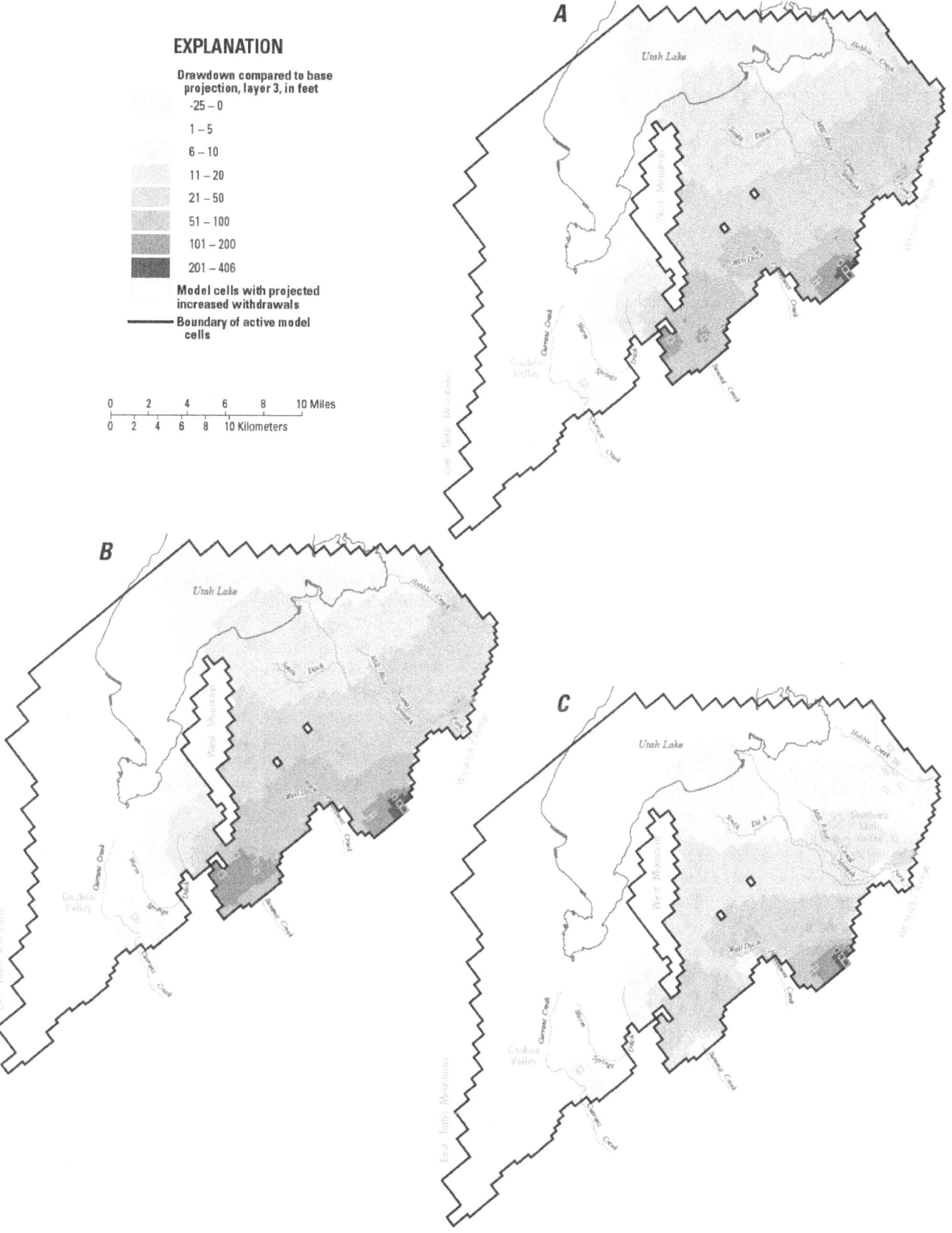

Figure 15. Drawdown compared to base projection for southern Utah and Goshen Valleys, Utah, in *A*, projection 2; *B*, projection 3; and *C*, projection 4.

Example Groundwater Management Simulations

Groundwater flow models can be combined with optimization techniques to determine water-resource management strategies that best meet a particular set of management objectives and constraints (Ahlfeld and others, 2005, p. 2). Optimization techniques are a set of mathematical programs that seek to find the optimal (or best) allocation of resources to competing uses. In the context of groundwater management, the resources are typically the groundwater and surface-water resources of a basin and the financial resources of the communities that depend on the water (Ahlfeld and others, 2005, p. 2). To demonstrate the utility of combining groundwater models with optimization models in southern Utah Valley, the computer program GWM-2005 (Ahlfeld and others, 2005) was used to simulate and solve groundwater management scenarios. A groundwater management formulation consists of decision variables, an objective function, and a set of constraints (Ahlfeld and others, 2005, p. 7). Decision variables are quantifiable controls that are determined by the model, such as the amount of pumping from each well or the amount of MAR at each location. The objective function is used to identify the best solution and is typically phrased as "maximize withdrawals", "minimize drawdown", or "minimize MAR". The constraints impose restrictions on the decision variables or state of the system, such as withdrawal at a well cannot exceed a certain amount, or drawdown cannot exceed a certain amount. The three examples described in this report are provided to illustrate the possible uses of GWM-2005 and are based on hypothetical and simplified decision variables and constraints. The water managers in the study area were not involved in setting these hypothetical values, nor are financial and engineering considerations included in these examples. To enable faster model simulations, the linear solution of GWM-2005 (Ahlfeld and others, 2005, p. 19) was used for these examples. This creates some error in the solution because of the non-linearities in the system, especially at head-dependent boundaries such as springs and streams, but is sufficient for the demonstration purposes of this report.

For these examples, decision variables in southern Utah Valley include how much water to withdraw from each area and how much, if any, MAR to apply in each area. Projected municipal withdrawals were either set at the estimated demand, or were maximized by GWM-2005 while meeting drawdown and spring discharge constraints. To minimize the number of decision variables, the individual wells were grouped into areas of municipal withdrawal, and the withdrawals from each area were used as decision variables (fig. 16). Also, to minimize the number of decision variables, the municipal withdrawals were assumed to increase in each period from 2012 to 2020, 2021 to 2030, 2031 to 2040, and 2041 to 2050, instead of annual increases (fig. 11). To provide optimum flexibility, the total projected municipal requirement was used rather than individual city requirements. The

maximum withdrawal from each well was constrained at 1,500 gal/min. MAR is allowed at locations discussed in the "Model Projections" section of this report and along the Strawberry Highline Canal (fig. 16). Maximum infiltration capacity is assumed to be 1,000 ft/yr on the basis of MAR infiltration rates in Arizona (Gorey and Dent, 2007), but the infiltration capacity in southern Utah Valley has not been analyzed by the USGS. This large capacity gives GWM-2005 the most flexibility in optimizing recharge locations. During simulations, the maximum infiltration capacity at MAR area MAPLE was reduced to about 380 ft/yr and the maximum infiltration capacity at MAR area PETEET was reduced to about 24 ft/yr to reduce simulated water-levels that would be above land surface.

The three examples of optimization presented in this report include constraints to groundwater withdrawals in southern Utah Valley by minimizing groundwater-level declines and minimizing the reduction in discharge to selected springs. Water levels were controlled in example 1 by maximizing simulated water levels at selected cells in four areas (fig. 17A) and in examples 2 and 3 by constraining simulated drawdown at selected model cells (fig. 17B). Additional constraints on water levels were used to prevent high water levels near MAR sites in example 3 (fig. 17B). Discharge to springs is constrained in example 1 by maximizing the smallest discharge to Salem Lake, Spring Lake, and springs near the fish hatchery in Springville. Discharge to springs in examples 2 and 3 is constrained by requiring a specified minimum discharge at each of those three springs (fig. 17B).

The first groundwater management example demonstrates the ability of GWM-2005 to determine withdrawal locations and amounts that allow for the highest possible water levels and spring discharge for a given withdrawal and no MAR. The objective function in GWM-2005 was to maximize the sum of the lowest water level in each of four areas (fig. 17A) and the smallest spring discharge. The constraints were that overall withdrawals must meet the expected demands in each decade (fig. 11). The effects of this example can be compared to projection 3, where municipal increases were applied at each well in each municipality. Example 1 indicates that maximum drawdown can be less than in projection 3 (fig. 18) and that spring discharge can be greater than in projection 3 at Salem Lake and Spring Lake (fig. 19) by withdrawing water mostly in the Springville, Mapleton, and Spanish Fork City areas (fig. 20).

The second groundwater management example demonstrates the ability of GWM-2005 to maximize withdrawals given constraints on drawdown and spring discharge. Constraints were that water levels at selected cells (fig. 17B) be no lower than 100 ft below the water level at the end of the base projection and that discharge to springs at Salem Lake, Spring Lake, and springs near the fish hatchery in Springville be at least 65 percent of the discharge at the end of the base projection. This example, which can also be compared to projection 3, indicates that about 92 percent of the projected demand can be supplied and meet these constraints (figs. 18C, 19, and 20).

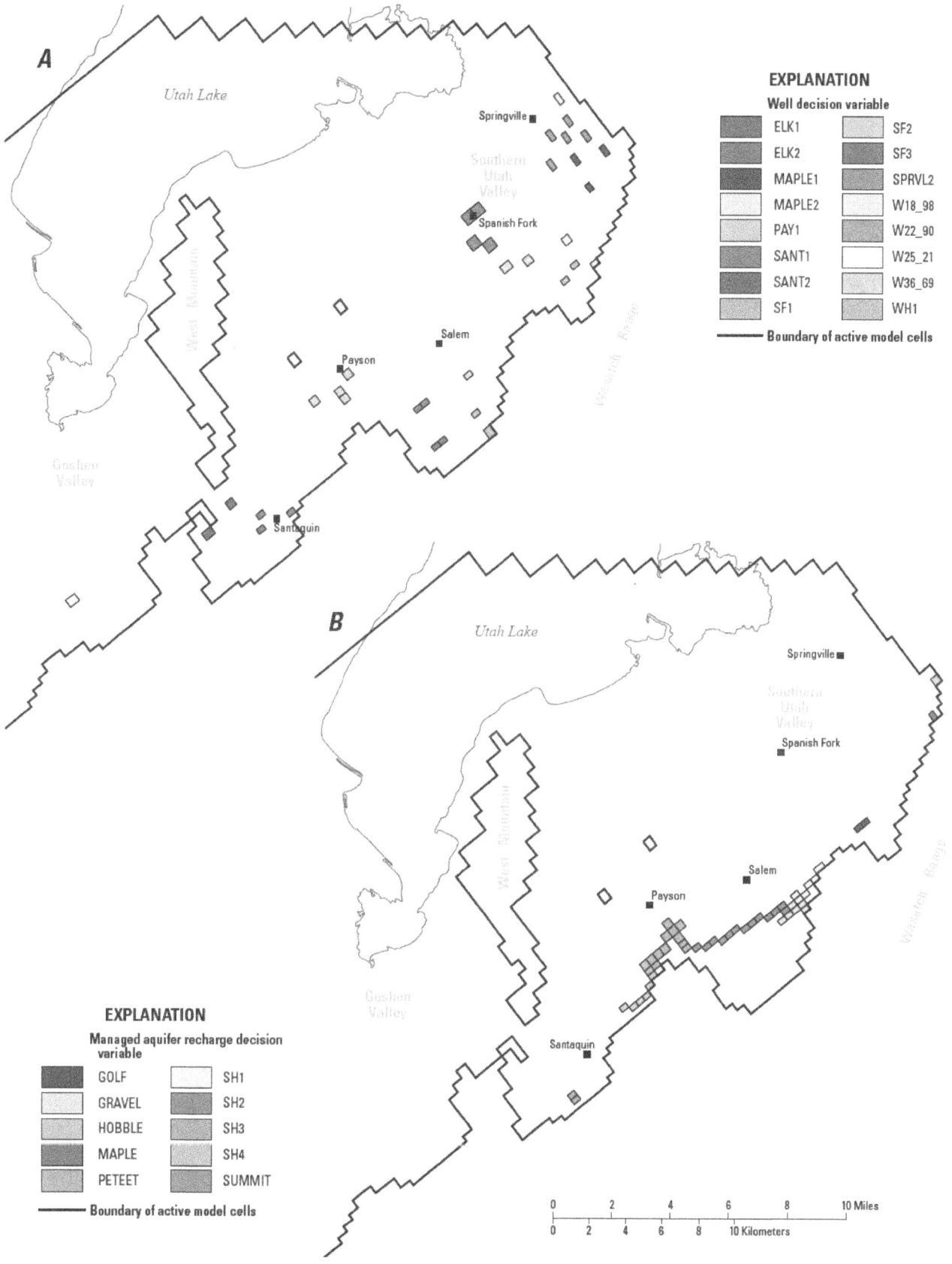

Figure 16. Location of well decision variables and managed aquifer recharge decision variables for optimization examples, southern Utah and Goshen Valleys, Utah.

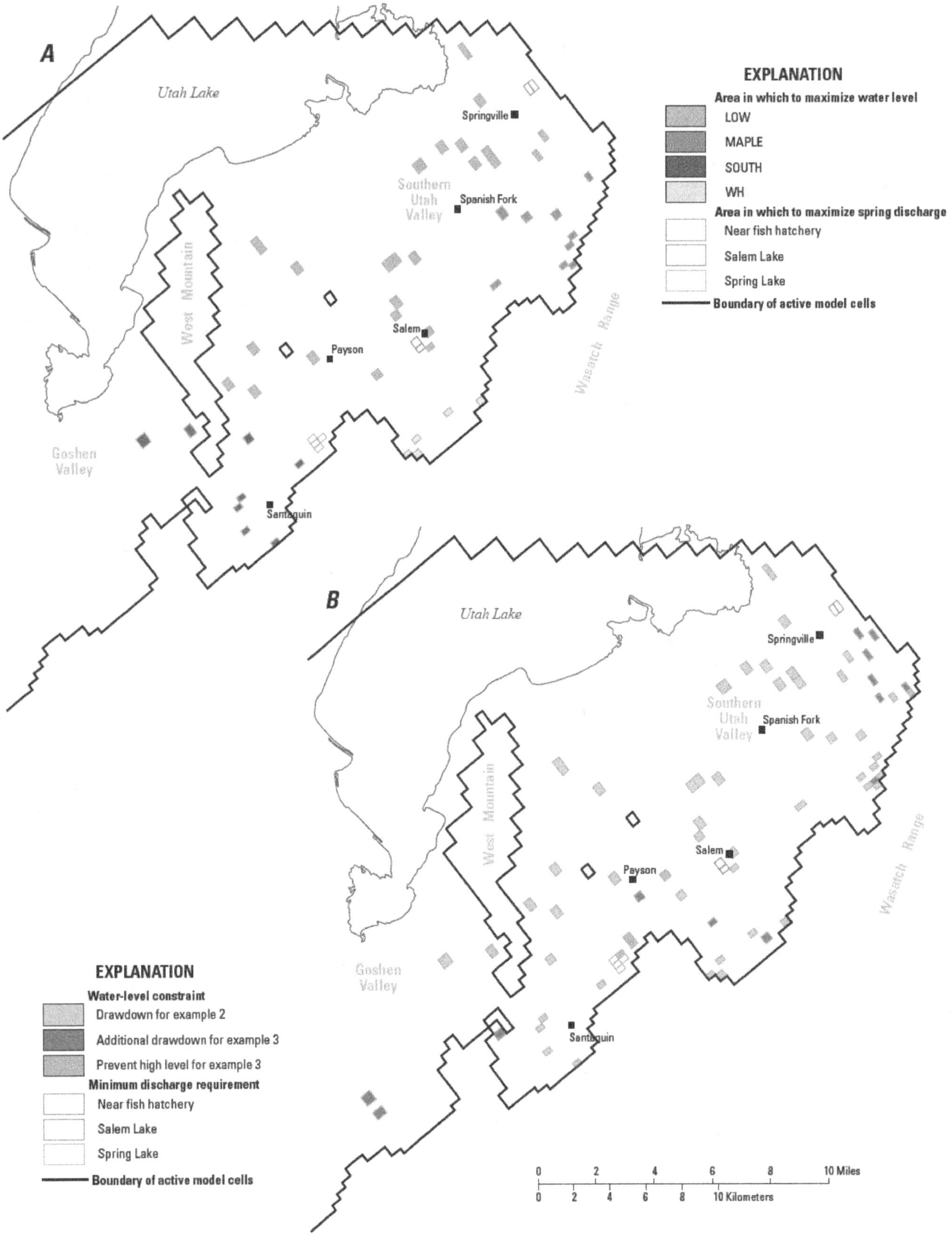

Figure 17. Locations in southern Utah and Goshen Valleys, Utah, of *A*, areas in which to maximize water levels and spring discharge and *B*, water-level and spring-discharge constraints for optimization examples.

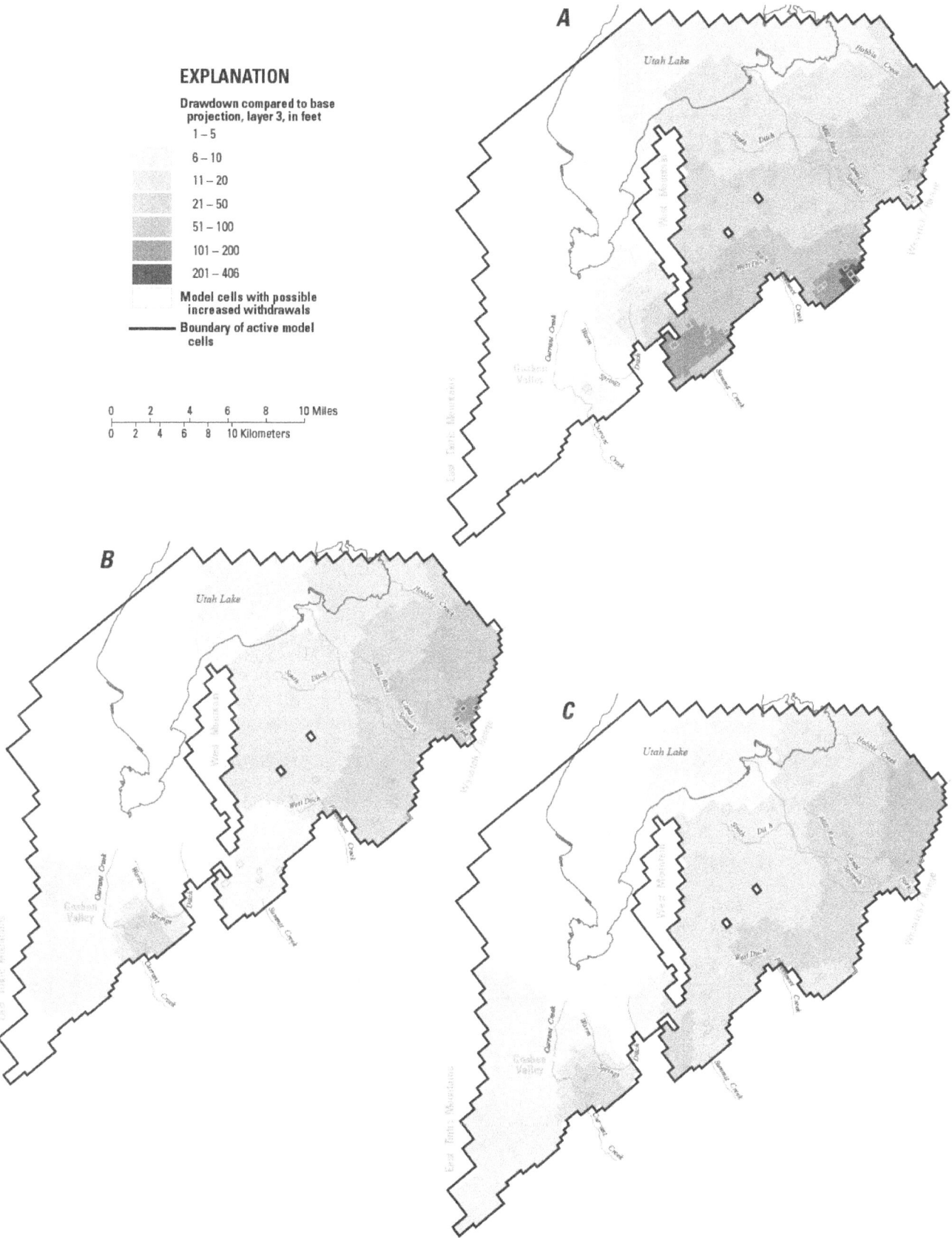

Figure 18. Drawdown compared to base projection for southern Utah and Goshen Valleys, Utah, in *A*, projection 3; *B*, optimization example 1; and *C*, optimization example 2.

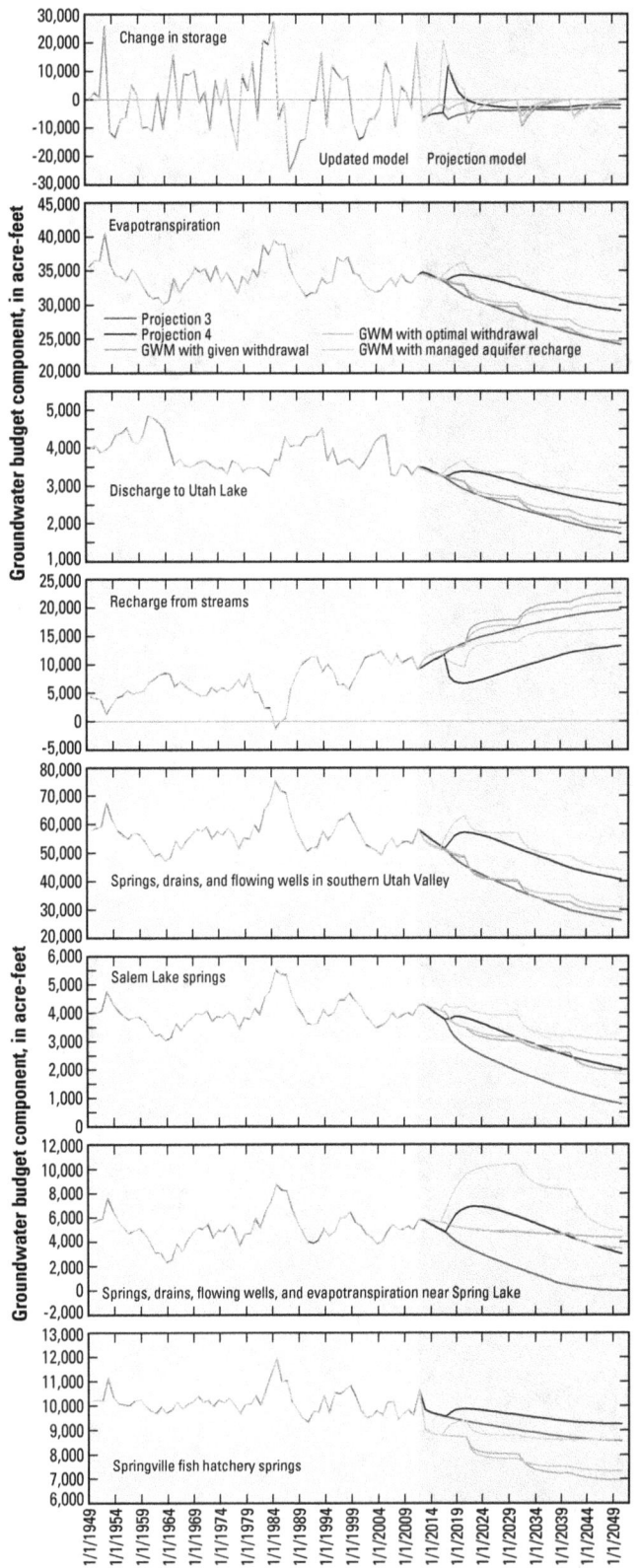

Because GWM-2005 was being run in linear mode, the final values of water levels and spring discharge are slightly less than the constraints in some areas.

The third groundwater management example illustrates combining well and MAR variables to maximize withdrawals if 30,000 acre-ft/yr of MAR were available. Constraints are that water levels in select cells (fig. 17B) be no lower than 20 ft below the water level simulated at the end of the base projection and that spring discharge at Salem Lake, Spring Lake, and the springs near the fish hatchery in Springville be at least 75 percent of the discharge at the end of the base projection. To limit rising water levels because of MAR, additional constraints are placed at select cells that do not allow the simulated water level in layer 1 to be higher than the simulated water level at the end of projection 1 or land surface minus 20 ft, whichever was highest (fig. 17B). This example can be compared to projection 4, and it illustrates that optimization of withdrawals and MAR can limit effects of increased withdrawals more efficiently than MAR without optimization (figs. 19 and 21). Because GWM-2005 was being run in linear mode, the final values of water levels are less than the constraints in some areas. The example also illustrates that withdrawals can be more evenly distributed throughout the municipalities by using optimization with MAR than by using optimization without MAR (fig. 20).

Figure 19. Selected simulated groundwater-budget components for optimization examples, southern Utah Valley, Utah.

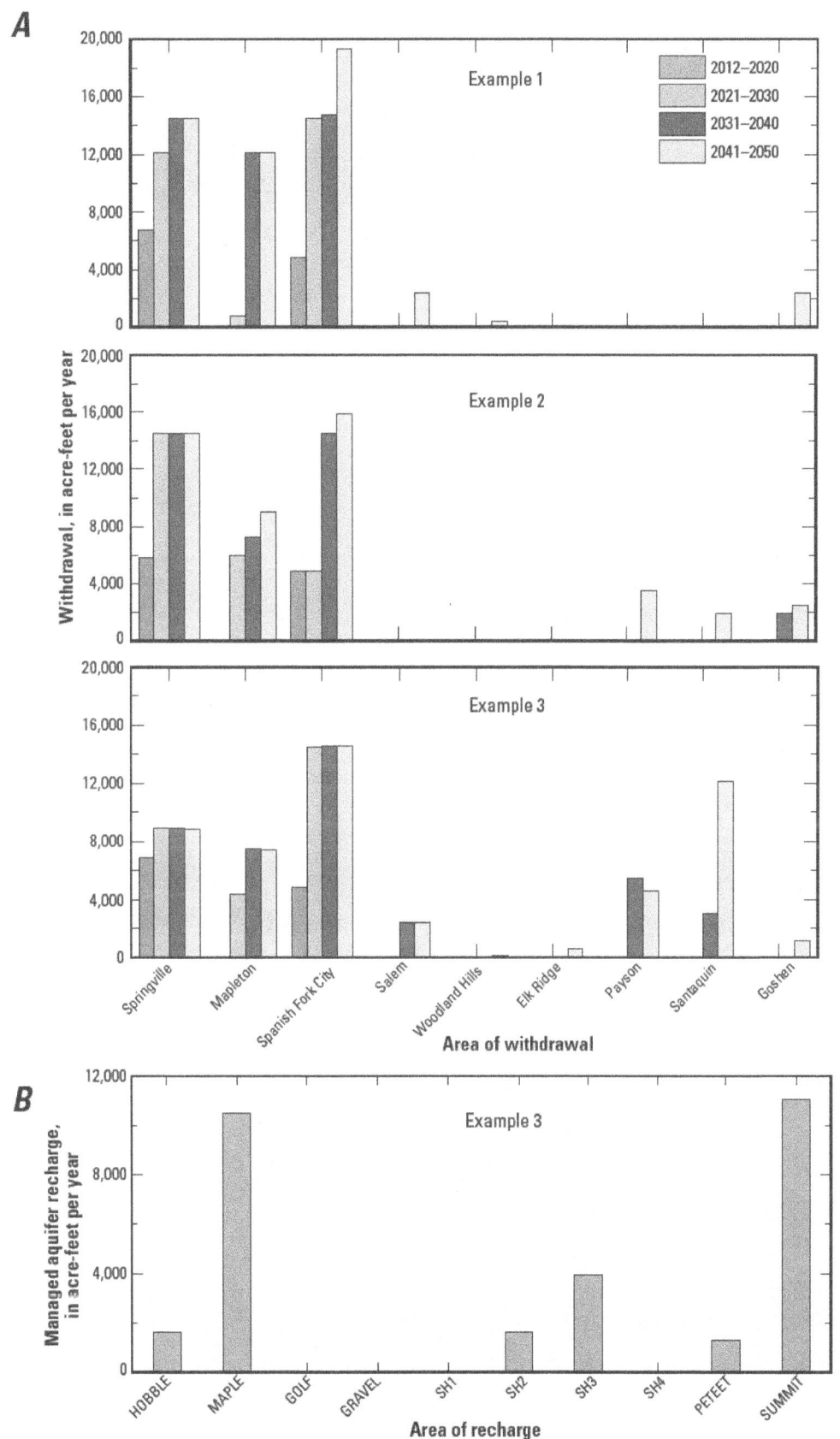

Figure 20. Amounts of groundwater withdrawals by area for optimization examples, southern Utah and Goshen Valleys, Utah.

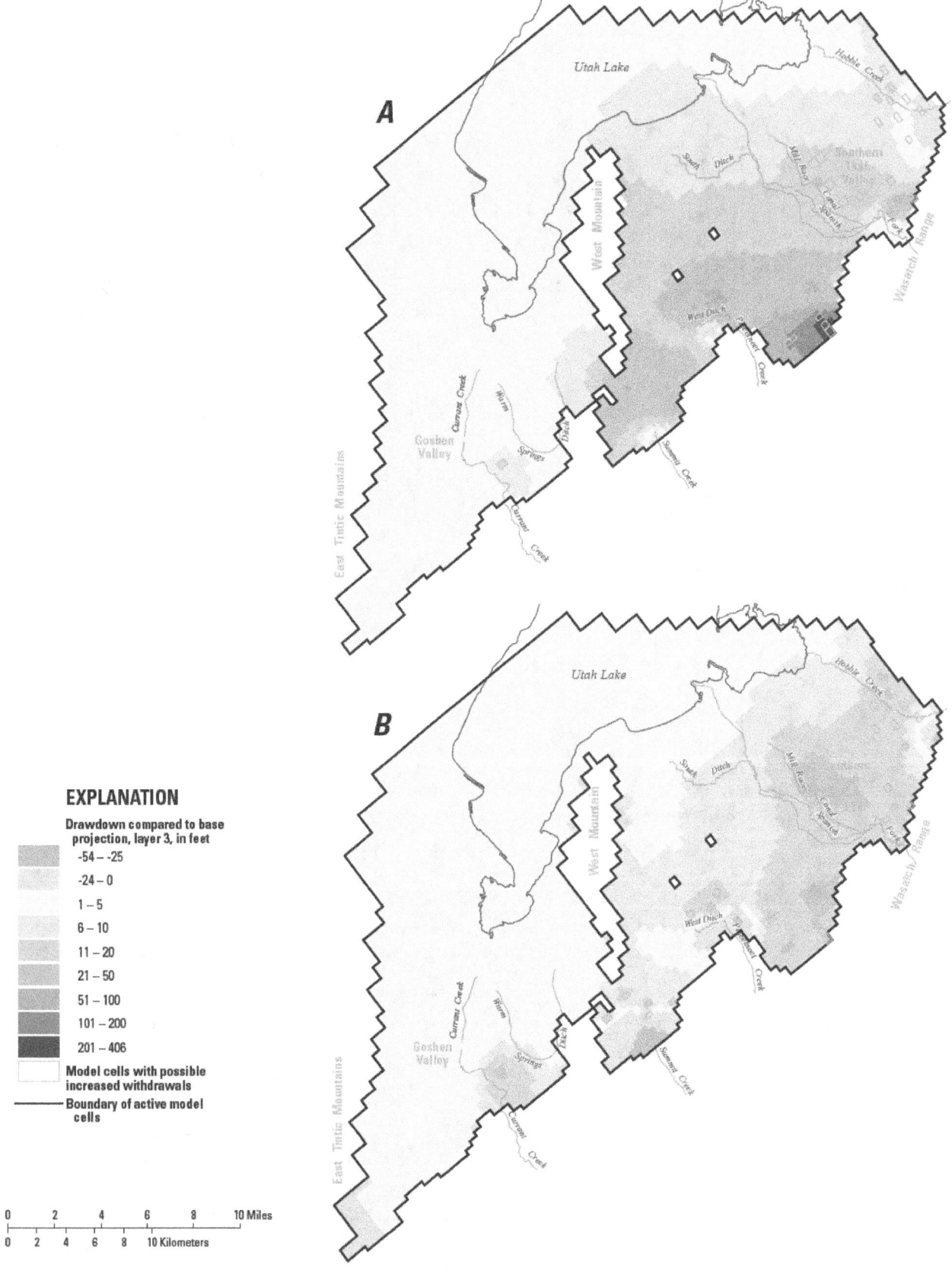

EXPLANATION

Drawdown compared to base projection, layer 3, in feet

-54 – -25
-24 – 0
1 – 5
6 – 10
11 – 20
21 – 50
51 – 100
101 – 200
201 – 406

Model cells with possible increased withdrawals

Boundary of active model cells

Figure 21.   Drawdown compared to base projection for southern Utah and Goshen Valleys, Utah, in A, projection 4 and B, optimization example 3.

Potential Revisions and New Data to Improve the Updated Model

Some revisions could be made to the model that may improve model fit to water-level changes and improve the accuracy of predictions without collecting new data. Recalibration to new stresses and available data may improve the confidence in model parameters and reduce the uncertainty in simulated predictions. The dramatic increase in groundwater withdrawals in southern Utah Valley from 1999 to 2000 caused a stress on the system outside the range of stresses during the calibration period. It is possible that transmissivity and storage properties could be changed in such a way that would allow the model to simulate more accurately the drawdown from March 2000 to March 2002. Changing from an annual stress period to a seasonal stress period may improve model fit if data are available to understand the system and calibrate the model on a seasonal basis. Many new wells are located close to Spanish Fork River or Hobble Creek (fig. 7), and the model predicts increasing recharge from streams with increased withdrawals. During the period of greatest withdrawals in summer, however, those streams do not have much flow and possibly could not recharge the groundwater system as much as is allowed during an annual stress period.

Model calibration could be further improved by collection of the following data: the flow in Spanish Fork River below the Power Canal diversion, the flow in Hobble Creek, seepage runs on Spanish Fork River and Hobble Creek, updated estimate of discharge to evapotranspiration, discharge to springs, and an updated estimate of discharge to large flowing wells. Additional data about stream-aquifer interactions could be obtained with shallow piezometers in the streambeds and measurements of temperature and chemical changes along the stream channels. An updated evaluation of land use, crop types, irrigation methods, and municipal water applied to lawns and gardens would allow recharge to be better simulated.

The model probably cannot be improved in Goshen Valley without additional data collection that includes the following: updated withdrawal locations and amounts, updated evaluation of crop types and irrigation methods, updated estimate of discharge to evapotranspiration, updated estimates of recharge from and discharge to Currant Creek and Currant Creek Canal, and updated information on the distribution of water from Warm Springs. After collection of the data, the model would need to be modified to account for the changes found, and aquifer properties would need to be recalibrated to represent the groundwater system more closely.

Additional improvements in the model could be made by using the methods available with MODFLOW-2005 (Harbaugh, 2005) and UCODE_2005 (Poeter and others, 2005) to estimate model parameters by using regression techniques. These techniques also provide a quantitative assessment of model and prediction uncertainty.

Summary

The U.S. Geological Survey (USGS), in cooperation with the Southern Utah Valley Municipal Water Association, updated an existing USGS model of southern Utah and Goshen Valleys for hydrologic and climatic conditions from 1991 to 2011. Increased withdrawals from 1999 to 2000 and below-average precipitation and streamflow in 2000 to 2003 caused water levels in many wells in the area to decline to their lowest recorded levels by 2005. The model was updated and evaluated to see if it could adequately simulate these conditions and to determine if the model is adequate for use in future planning.

All model files used in the transient model were updated to be compatible with MODFLOW-2005 and with the additional stress periods. The well and recharge files had the most extensive changes. Discharge to pumping wells in southern Utah and Goshen Valleys was estimated and simulated on an annual basis from 1991 to 2011. New wells (since 1990) are concentrated in the Spanish Fork and Springville area, the Santaquin area, and central Goshen Valley. Recharge estimates for 1991 to 2011 were included in the updated model by using precipitation, streamflow, canal diversions, and irrigation groundwater withdrawals for each year.

In southern Utah Valley, the magnitude and direction of annual water-level fluctuations simulated by the updated model reasonably match measured water-level changes. The similar response indicates that the variation in annual recharge and annual withdrawals simulated in the model are generally good approximations of the actual changes in the groundwater system. In several areas, however, the model does not simulate as much decline as was measured from 2000 to 2002. Both the rapid increase in withdrawals and the total withdrawals in southern Utah Valley during this period exceed changes and amounts in the calibration period; it is possible that hydraulic properties may be locally incorrect and allow changes in simulated natural discharge that do not happen as rapidly in the groundwater system. It is also possible that other changes in the system that are not simulated contributed to the steep groundwater-level decline; these could include differences in streamflow, differences in land use and irrigation, or other causes. The model reasonably simulates water-level changes in southern Utah Valley after 2002.

In the northern part of Goshen Valley, simulated water-level changes reasonably match measured changes. Farther south, however, simulated declines are much less than measured declines, even though in the transient calibration period, simulated changes reasonably matched measured changes. Land-use changes indicate it is possible that groundwater withdrawals in Goshen Valley are greater than estimated. It is also possible that groundwater withdrawal during the calibration period did not cause enough stress to determine accurate hydraulic properties of the aquifer.

The model can be used for projections about the effects of future groundwater withdrawals and applied recharge water in southern Utah Valley. Rapid changes may not be simulated correctly, and increasing withdrawals dramatically may reduce the accuracy of the predicted water-level and groundwater budget changes. The model should not be used for projections in Goshen Valley until additional withdrawal and discharge data are collected and the model is recalibrated, if necessary. Recalibration to new stresses and seasonal stress periods, and collection of new withdrawal, stream, land-use, and discharge data could improve the model and the accuracy of predictions.

For three projections with increased withdrawals, the maximum drawdown from the base projection with no increase in withdrawals is about 400 ft. In projection 3, with increased withdrawals and piping of the Strawberry Highline Canal, some areas of natural discharge no longer discharge groundwater. Projection 4, with managed aquifer recharge (MAR), reduces the effects of increased withdrawals and has less area with large water-level declines and less reduction in natural discharge than the other projections with increased withdrawals. Optimization examples indicate that groundwater-level declines can be less and discharge to select springs can be greater by optimizing the location of withdrawals and MAR.

References

Ahlfeld, D.P., Barlow, P.M., and Mulligan, A.E., 2005, GWM—A ground-water management process for the U.S. Geological Survey modular ground-water model (MOD-FLOW-2000): U.S. Geological Survey Open-File Report 2005–1072, 124 p.

Brooks, L.E., and Stolp, B.J., 1995, Hydrology and simulation of ground-water flow in southern Utah and Goshen Valleys, Utah: Utah Department of Natural Resources Technical Publication No. 111, 96 p.

Burden, C.B., and others, 2012, Groundwater conditions in Utah, spring of 2012: Utah Department of Natural Resources Cooperative Investigations Report No. 53, 118 p.

Gorey, Timothy, and Dent, Patrick, 2007, Maintenance techniques utilized by Central Arizona Project to optimize recharge *in* Fox, Peter, ed., Management of aquifer recharge for sustainability: Phoenix, Ariz., Acacia Publishing Inc., p. 404–411.

Harbaugh, A.W., 2005, MODFLOW-2005, the U.S. Geological Survey modular ground-water model—The groundwater flow process: U.S. Geological Survey Techniques and Methods 6–A16, variously p.

Hely, A.G, Mower, R.W., and Harr, C.A., 1971, Water resources of Salt Lake County, Utah: Utah Department of Natural Resources Technical Publication 31, 240 p.

Konikow, L.F., and Bredehoft, J.D., 1992, Ground-water models cannot be validated: Advances in Water Resources, v. 15, No. 1, p. 75–83.

Leake, S.A., and Prudic, D.E., 1991, Documentation of a computer program to simulate aquifer-system compaction using the modular finite-difference ground-water flow model: U.S. Geological Techniques of Water-Resources Investigation Book 6, Chapter A2, variously paged.

McDonald, M.G., and Harbaugh, A.W., 1988, A modular three-dimensional finite-difference ground-water flow model: U.S. Geological Survey Techniques of Water Resources Investigations, Book 6, Chapter A1, variously paged.

Poeter, E.P., Hill, M.C., Banta, E.R., Mehl, Steffen, and Christensen, Steen, 2005, UCODE_2005 and six other computer codes for universal sensitivity analysis, calibration, and uncertainty evaluation: U.S. Geological Survey Techniques and Methods 6–A11, 283 p.

Prudic, D.E., 1989, Documentation of a computer program to simulate stream-aquifer relations using a modular, finite-difference, ground-water flow model: U.S. Geological Survey Open-File Report 88–729, 113 p.

Richardson, G.B., 1906, Underground water in the valleys of Utah Lake and Jordan River, Utah: U.S. Geological Survey Water-Supply and Irrigation Paper No. 157, 81 p.

U.S. Geological Survey, 2012, USGS Surface-Water Annual Statistics for Utah: accessed on September 28, 2012, at *http://waterdata.usgs.gov/ut/nwis/annual?site_no=10150500&agency_cd=USGS&referred_module=sw&format=sites_selection_links*.

Utah Division of Water Rights, 2012a, Water Records and Use Information Viewer: accessed multiple times from April to September 2012 at *http://www.waterrights.utah.gov/cgi-bin/wuseview.exe?Startup*.

Utah Division of Water Rights, 2012b, River Commissioner Records Viewer: accessed multiple times from April to September 2012 at *http://www.waterrights.utah.gov/cgi-bin/dvrtview.exe?Startup*.

Western Regional Climate Center, 2012a, Payson, Utah (426724), Monthly Climate Summary: accessed on May 9, 2012, at *http://www.wrcc.dri.edu/cgi-bin/cliMAIN.pl?ut6724*.

Western Regional Climate Center, 2012b, Santaquin Chlorinator, Utah (427686) Monthly Climate Summary: accessed on May 9, 2012, at *http://www.wrcc.dri.edu/cgi-bin/cliMAIN.pl?ut7686*.

Appendix 1: Supplemental Groundwater Management Simulation

An additional groundwater management simulation was completed at the request of the cooperator. Because the report was already in review, this additional simulation is described in this appendix. The objective of the simulation was to minimize managed aquifer recharge (MAR) while meeting specific constraints. The locations and amounts of MAR, the amount of increased withdrawals, and the guidelines for drawdown, spring discharge, and high water levels were provided by Caldwell, Richards, Sorensen (CRS) Engineers, the representative of the cooperator.

Decision Variables and Constraints

The only decision variables in this optimization simulation are the locations and amounts of MAR. To provide an estimate of when MAR would be required in each area, the MAR decision variables were assigned by decade; this is similar to how withdrawals were assigned in the other optimization simulations described in this report. Five locations for possible MAR were provided by the cooperator (fig. A1-1); each can have a different recharge rate, up to the maximum at each site, for each of the four decades of the simulation. The maximum amount of MAR is 58,000 acre-ft/yr, but this maximum would only be simulated if the MAR in each area was maximized. Unused MAR at one location would not be available at another location. From north to south, the maximum amounts, in acre-ft/yr, are as follows: HBBLE, 4,000; HWY89, 15,000; GRVEL, 15,000; PTEET, 12,000; SMMIT, 12,000.

For the example groundwater management simulations presented in this report, the municipal demand could be supplied from any well in any city up to a maximum amount per well. The cooperator desired that for the groundwater management simulation presented in this appendix, the projected demands be kept in each city; as a result of this, the increased withdrawals were removed as decision variables in this simulation and are considered as a specified discharge at the location of the existing wells. This is the same method and amount of withdrawal as used in the projection simulations described in this report, but it limits the ability of optimization to determine the best withdrawal locations.

The objective function in this simulation minimizes the total amount of MAR applied during the simulation. Because of this, constraints are set at the end of each decade to ensure that the simulation does not allow undesirable conditions in early decades and apply enough MAR during the last decade to meet the constraints only at the end of the simulation. Constraints are used to define the maximum changes in the system that are acceptable to water users and communities in the area. The following constraints are applied throughout southern Utah Valley (fig. A1-1):

1. The constraint for drawdown is 50 ft for most of the modeled area. Discussions with the cooperator clarified that this would not be possible in all areas given the other constraints on withdrawal locations and high water levels near recharge areas. Drawdown is calculated as the difference between simulated levels at the end of projection 1 (base case with average recharge with no increase in withdrawals) and levels simulated during the optimization.

2. The constraint for discharge to Salem Pond, Spring Lake and surrounding area, and the springs near the fish hatchery in Springville are that rates are not be reduced more than 10 percent from the simulated discharge at the end of projection 1. Discussions with the cooperator clarified that it might not be possible for optimization to obtain a solution that minimizes changes in discharge in the Spring Lake area while not allowing high levels in the recharge area south of Payson (area PTEET). If a solution was not possible, the spring constraint was adjusted to a lower amount to allow optimization.

3. Water-level rises are limited to prevent flooding. The following criteria were used to minimize high water levels:

   a. In many parts of the study area and the model, water levels are within 20 ft of land surface with the current hydrologic conditions. In areas where the simulated water level at the end of projection 1 is within 20 ft of land surface, the constraint is that water levels not rise above that level.

   b. In areas where the simulated water level at the end of projection 1 is lower than 20 ft below land surface, the constraint is that water levels cannot rise above 20 ft below land surface.

Results

The maximum total MAR for this simulation is about 33,000 acre-ft/yr. MAR in areas HBBLE and GRVEL is at the maximum amount allowed in each area in the final decade of the simulation. MAR is limited in areas HWY89 and PTEET because water levels would rise too high with greater recharge rates. As a result, drawdowns exceed 50 ft in parts of Payson, in one cell with a withdrawal well near Mill Race Canal, and in one cell with a withdrawal well near the mouth of Spanish Fork Canyon (fig. A1-2). Because MAR is limited by the high water levels south of Payson, the discharge in the Spring Lake area cannot be maintained at 90 percent of the flow in projection 1 and is reduced to about 70 percent of the flow by the end of the simulation (fig. A1-3). The amounts of recharge at each MAR area generally increase with each decade, but

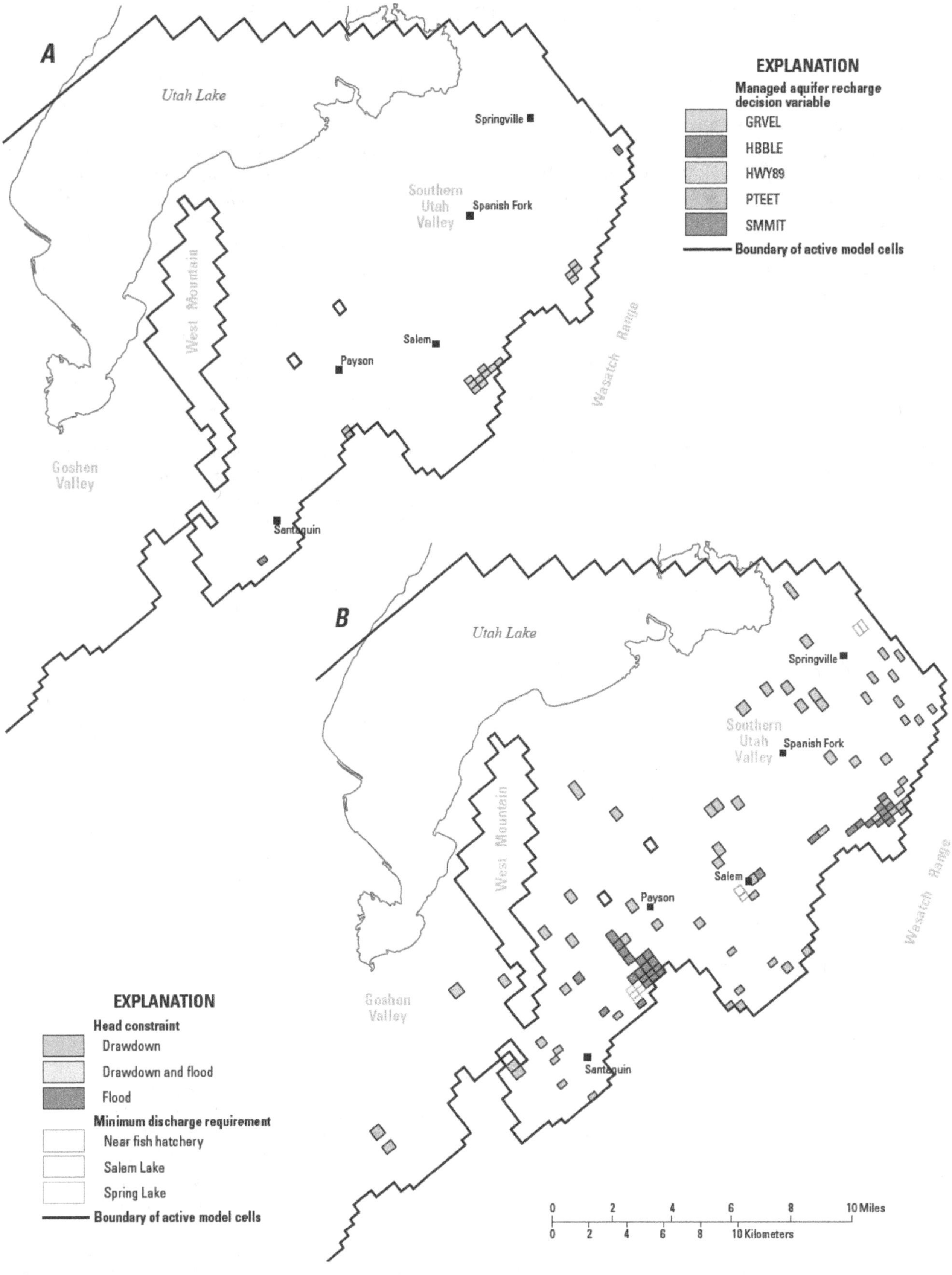

Figure A1-1. Location in southern Utah and Goshen Valleys, Utah, of *A*, managed aquifer recharge decision variables and *B*, water-level and spring-discharge constraints.

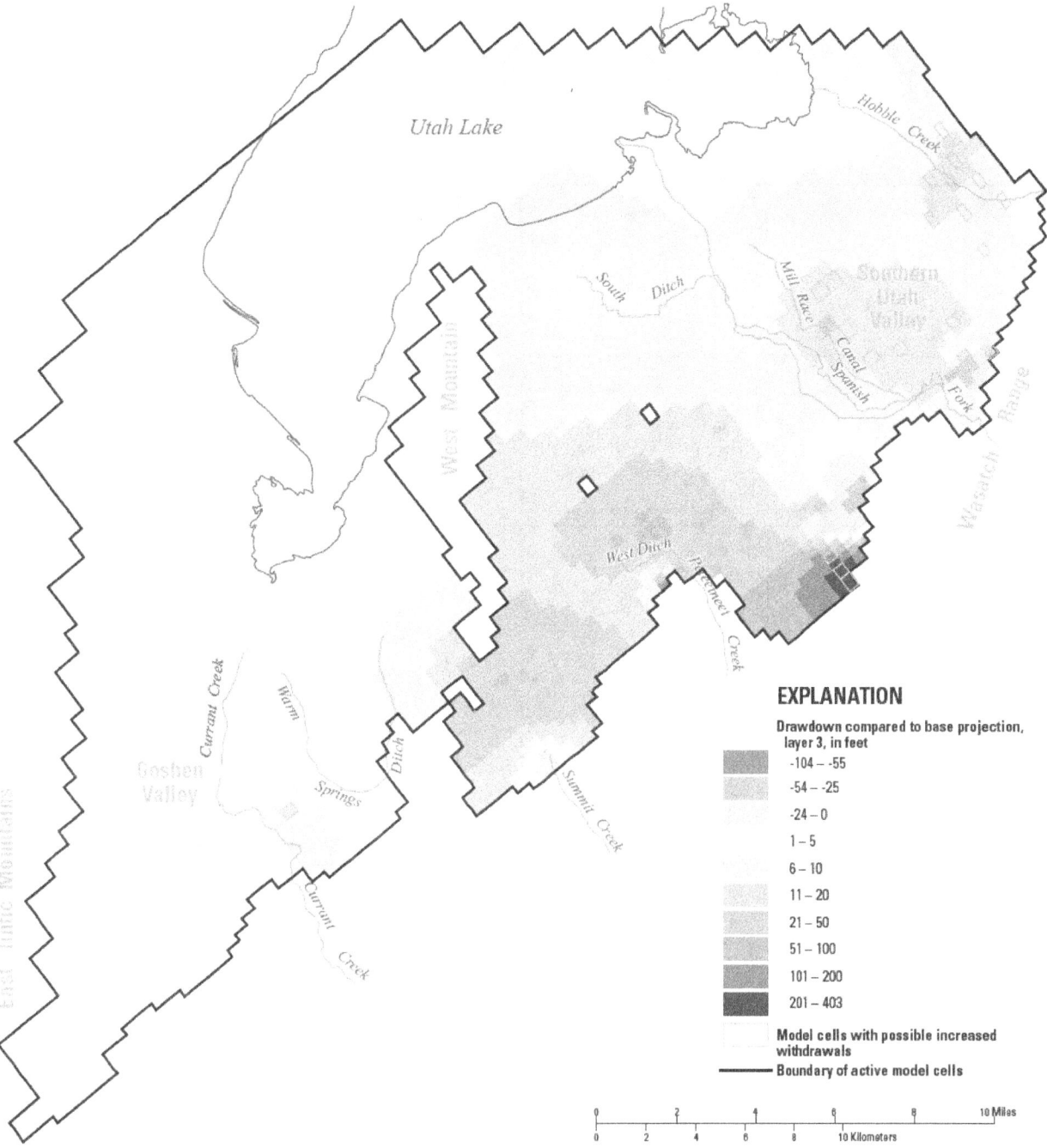

Figure A1-2. Drawdown compared to base projection, southern Utah and Goshen Valleys, Utah.

there are exceptions (fig. A1-4). Detailed examination of GWM-2005 (Ahlfeld and others, 2005) output files indicates that more than one recharge scenario involving the areas south of Payson and near Santaquin will meet the constraints posed in this problem. To a certain extent, recharge at the area south of Payson can be replaced by recharge near Santaquin and satisfy the constraints. A more detailed analysis involving preferred recharge areas, costs of recharge for each area, or different water-level and spring-flow discharge constraints could provide a unique solution, but was outside the scope of this project.

The constraints on high water levels prevent determining how much MAR would be required to meet the drawdown constraints in Payson and near the mouth of Spanish Fork Canyon; it may be less than or more than 58,000 acre-ft/yr. Because the objective, constraints, and decision variables are different in this simulation than in the example optimization simulations, direct comparisons of the results cannot be made.

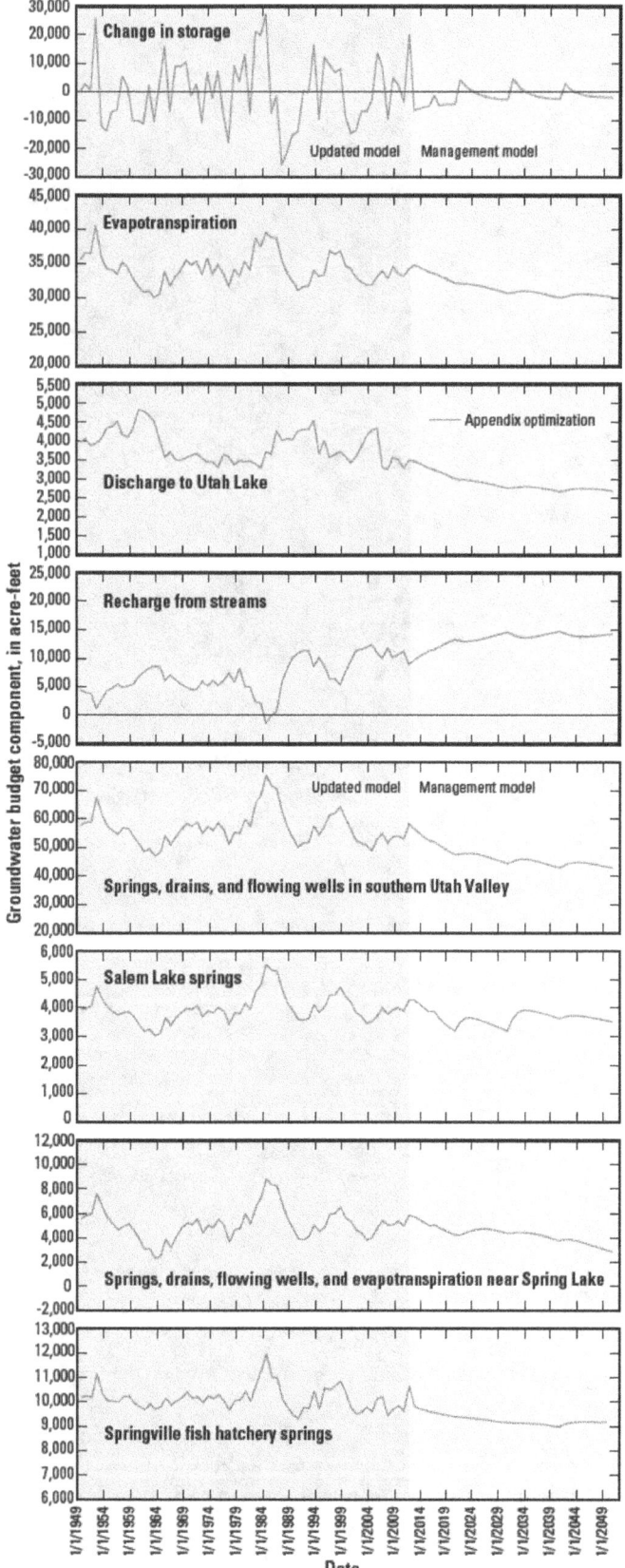

Figure A1-3.   Selected simulated groundwater-budget components, southern Utah Valley, Utah.

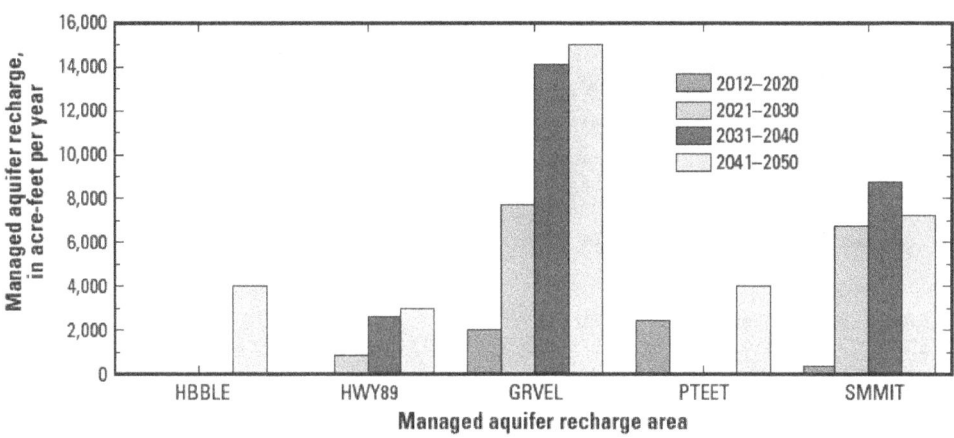

Figure A1-4.   Amounts of optimized managed aquifer recharge by area, southern Utah Valley, Utah.